Old Fashioned
COUNTRY
COOKING

Old Fashioned COUNTRY COOKING

Julia M. Pitkin, Editor

RUTLEDGE HILL PRESS
NASHVILLE, TENNESSEE

Illustrations by Tonya Pitkin, Studio III Productions.

Published in Nashville, Tennessee, by Rutledge Hill Press, Inc., 513 Third Avenue South, Nashville, Tennessee 37210.

Typography by Bailey Typography, Inc., Nashville, Tennessee.

Library of Congress Cataloging-in-Publication Data

Old-fashioned country cooking.

   Includes index.
   1.   Cookery, American—Southern style.   I. Pitkin,
Julia M.
TX715.2.S68043   1988   641.5975   88-23936
ISBN 0-93495-85-3

Printed in the United States of America
3 4 5 6 7 8 — 94 93 92 91

Contents

■ ■ ■ ■ ■ ■ ■ ■

Old Fashioned
COUNTRY
COOKING

Recipes featured on the cover:

Flannel Cakes, page 9
Baked Ham, page 14
Stewed Okra and Tomatoes, page 82
Acorn Squash with Peas, page 86
Jam-Filled Corn Muffins, page 93
Corn Sticks, page 94

Menus

■ ■ ■ ■ ■ ■

Breakfast in the Country

Flannel Cakes
Thick Country Smoked Bacon
Pure Whole Butter and Real Maple Syrup
Hot Apple Cider Punch

FLANNEL CAKES
2 to 4 servings

2 egg whites
1 cup all-purpose flour
1 tablespoon baking
   powder
½ teaspoon salt

2 tablespoons sugar
2 egg yolks
1 cup milk
2 tablespoons hot bacon
   grease

■ Beat the egg whites until stiff. In a separate bowl sift together the flour, baking powder, salt, and sugar. In a small bowl beat the egg yolks with the milk. Stir the milk mixture into the dry ingredients. Gently fold in the beaten egg whites. When smooth, fold in the bacon grease. Cook the pancakes on a hot griddle.

Hot Apple Cider Punch

4 cups apple cider
2 6-ounce cans frozen
   lemonade concentrate,
   thawed

2 cups water
8 cinnamon sticks
Lemon slices

■ Into a large saucepan pour the cider, lemonade concentrate, and water; stir. Over medium heat bring the cider to a simmer. Pour into cups. Place a cinnamon stick and a slice of lemon in each cup.

Scrambled Eggs Breakfast

Broccoli-Cheese Scrambled Eggs
Center Cut Country Ham
Biscuits or Toast
Apple Oatmeal Crisp
Spiced Lemon Tea

Broccoli-Cheese Scrambled Eggs
4 servings

8 eggs, beaten
4 tablespoons milk
   Salt and pepper to taste
2 tablespoons margarine

1 cup shredded Cheddar
   cheese
½ cup chopped cooked
   broccoli

■ Stir together the eggs, milk, salt, and pepper. In a frying pan melt the margarine and add the egg mixture. Add the cheese and broccoli, and scramble together. Serve hot.

APPLE OATMEAL CRISP
9 servings

4 cups thinly sliced tart
  apples
1½ tablespoons lemon juice
3½ tablespoons sugar
⅓ cup all-purpose flour
1 cup rolled oats

½ cup packed brown sugar
1 teaspoon cinnamon
1 cup chopped walnuts
½ teaspoon salt
½ cup melted butter

■ Butter a 9-inch square pan. Toss the apples with the lemon juice and sugar, and place in the pan. Combine the remaining ingredients and sprinkle over the apples. Bake at 375° for 35 minutes.

SPICED LEMON TEA MIX
2 cups dry mix

1 cup instant tea powder with
  lemon
1 cup sugar

2 teaspoons ground cloves
2 teaspoons ground ginger
1 teaspoon ground allspice

■ Combine all of the ingredients and mix well. Store in an airtight container.
    To make 1 serving, place 3 tablespoons of tea mix in a mug and add 1 cup of boiling water. Stir until blended.

Country Lunch for Company

Skillet Chicken Stew
Biscuits or Rolls
Jellies and Honey
Fresh Fruits

SKILLET CHICKEN STEW
4 servings

3 tablespoons butter
1 frying chicken, cut up
¼ pound small mushrooms
4 carrots, thickly sliced
2 stalks celery, cut into
pieces
1 pound small red
potatoes, quartered

1 14½-ounce can chicken
broth
1 teaspoon salt
¼ teaspoon thyme leaves
2 tablespoons water
4 teaspoons all-purpose
flour

■ Melt the butter in a large skillet. Cook the chicken, a few pieces at a time, until browned. In the drippings, cook the mushrooms, carrots, and celery over medium heat until browned. Add the potatoes, chicken broth, salt, and thyme. Return the chicken to the skillet and heat to boiling. Reduce the heat to low and cover. Simmer for 30 minutes, stirring occasionally, until the chicken is tender.

Skim the fat from the liquid in the skillet. In a cup combine the flour and water, and stir into the skillet. Bring to a boil, stirring until thickened. Serve.

BAKING POWDER BISCUITS
12 biscuits

2 cups sifted all-purpose flour
2 teaspoons baking powder

1 teaspoon salt
¼ cup cold shortening
⅔ cup cold milk

■ Sift the flour, baking powder, and salt together and cut in the shortening with 2 knives or a pastry blender. Add the milk and mix quickly. Knead for a few seconds on a lightly floured board. Pat out to ½-inch thickness and cut with a biscuit cutter. For soft sides, place close together on a greased baking sheet. For crusty sides, place apart. Bake at once at 450° for 12 minutes.

Country Picnic Lunch

Bacon, Lettuce, and Tomato Sandwiches
Fresh Corn Soup
Sweet Potato Salad

FRESH CORN SOUP
8 servings

14 ears corn	*2 teaspoons salt*
2 cups water	*½ teaspoon pepper*
2 cups milk	*Chopped chives*
1 cup half and half	

■ Cut the corn kernels from the ears into a pan. Scrape any remaining corn and juice from the ears. Add the water and cook over medium heat for 5 to 10 minutes, until soft. With a slotted spoon remove 1 cup of corn. Puree the remaining corn. In a large bowl combine the pureed corn, milk, half and half, reserved corn, salt and pepper. Serve chilled or at room temperature. Garnish with chives.

SWEET POTATO SALAD
8 servings

3 pounds sweet potatoes	*¼ teaspoon pepper*
¼ cup lime juice	*¾ cup oil*
¾ teaspoon ground cumin	*¼ cup chopped parsley*
¾ teaspoon salt	

■ Peel the potatoes and cut into chunks. Cook in boiling water for 15 to 20 minutes, until tender. Drain. Stir together the lime juice, cumin, salt, and pepper. Whisk in the oil. Toss the potatoes with the dressing. Sprinkle parsley over all. Serve chilled or at room temperature.

Family Reunion Dinner

Baked Ham
Poppy Seed Muffins
Collard and Mustard Greens with Bacon
Southern Fried Apples
Strawberry Shortcake

BAKED HAM

Cooked boneless ham
Whole cloves
1½ cups brown sugar
2 cups pineapple juice
1 tablespoon mustard
2 cups diced pineapple
Ginger ale

■ Stud the ham with the cloves. In a blender combine the next 4 ingredients. Pour over the ham. Bake at 350° for 1 hour. Reduce the heat to 300° and bake for 2 hours. As the pan juices cook down, add ginger ale. Baste the ham every 15 minutes, adding ginger ale as needed.

POPPY SEED MUFFINS
2 dozen muffins

2½ cups sugar
2 cups evaporated milk
5 eggs
½ cup milk
5 cups all-purpose flour
4½ teaspoons baking powder
½ teaspoon salt
½ cup poppy seeds
1½ teaspoons vanilla extract

■ Combine the sugar, evaporated milk, eggs, and milk. In a separate bowl sift together the flour, baking powder, and salt. Add the milk mixture to the dry ingredients, and add the poppy seeds and vanilla. Beat until smooth. Pour into greased muffin cups. Bake at 350° for 40 minutes. Serve warm.

COLLARD AND MUSTARD GREENS

8 servings

4 ounces slab bacon,
    chopped
1 small onion, minced
2 large bunches collard
    greens, stemmed

1 bunch mustard greens,
    stemmed
½ cup chicken stock
    Salt and pepper
    Hot pepper sauce,
    optional

■ Cook the bacon in a large heavy skillet over medium heat. Reduce the heat to low and add the onion. Cook for 10 minutes until soft, stirring occasionally. Add the greens and stock. Cover and cook for about 25 minutes, stirring occasionally, until the greens are just tender. Season with salt and pepper. Sprinkle with hot sauce if desired.

SOUTHERN FRIED APPLES

6 servings

⅓ cup sugar
1 teaspoon nutmeg
½ teaspoon cinnamon

⅛ teaspoon salt
4 large cooking apples
5 tablespoons butter

■ Combine the sugar, nutmeg, cinnamon, and salt. Wash, core, and slice the apples into ½-inch thick rings. Heat the butter in a frying pan. Add the apple rings and half of the sugar mixture. Cook for about 3 minutes. Turn the apples, and sprinkle with the remaining sugar mixture. Cook until the apples are almost transparent. Serve hot.

Strawberry Shortcake
8 servings

3 cups all-purpose flour	½ cup shortening
3 teaspoons baking powder	1 egg, well beaten
½ teaspoon salt	1 cup milk
2 tablespoons sugar	1½ pints strawberries

■ Sift the flour with the baking powder, salt, and sugar. Cut in the shortening with two knives. Add the egg and milk, and blend well. The dough should be a soft one. Divide the dough in half and roll into rectangles approximately 9x13 inches. Place the rectangles in 2 greased pans. Bake at 400° until light golden in color.

Mash 1 cup of strawberries and sweeten to taste. Spread the mashed strawberries over one layer of shortcake, and top with the other layer. Sweeten the remaining strawberries, reserving a few for garnish, and arrange over the top layer. Cover with whipped cream, and garnish with whole strawberries.

Country Pork Dinner

Baked Fresh Pork Butt
Cornmeal-Chive Biscuits
Vegetable Fritters
Blueberry Buckle

Baked fresh pork butt

■ Select a fresh pork butt of the desired size. Rinse well under cool water. Place on a rack in a roasting pan, and add 2 cups of water. Cover. Bake at 350° for 40 minutes per pound. Remove the butt from the oven. Excellent served cold.

Cornmeal-chive biscuits
6 biscuits

1½ cups all-purpose flour
½ cup yellow cornmeal
1 tablespoon baking powder
1 teaspoon granulated sugar
½ teaspoon salt

⅓ cup shortening, at room temperature
3 tablespoons snipped fresh chives
2 teaspoons minced fresh oregano
⅔ cup milk

■ In a large bowl mix together the flour, cornmeal, baking powder, sugar, and salt. Cut in the shortening until the mixture resembles coarse meal. Mix in the chives and oregano. Add the milk and stir with a fork just until a soft dough forms. Turn out onto a floured board; knead gently 10 times or until smooth. Pat into a circle about 1-inch thick and cut into 2½-inch rounds. Gather the scraps, knead and pat to cut enough more rounds to make 6 biscuits. Arrange on an ungreased cookie sheet. Bake at 425° for 15 minutes or until golden. Serve warm.

Vegetable Fritters
18 fritters

½ cup all-purpose flour
½ teaspoon baking powder
½ teaspoon salt
¼ teaspoon pepper
1 egg

¼ cup milk
2 tablespoons oil
1 cup grated carrots
½ cup grated zucchini
2 green onions, sliced

■ Combine the flour, baking powder, salt, and pepper. In a separate bowl beat together the egg, milk, carrot, zucchini, and green onion. Stir the wet ingredients into the dry until just combined. Heat 1 tablespoon of oil in a skillet. Pour the batter by tablespoons into the hot oil. Cook until golden, about 2 minutes on each side. Add the remaining oil to the skillet as needed.

Blueberry Buckle
9 servings

½ cup shortening
½ cup sugar
1 egg, well beaten
2 cups all-purpose flour, sifted
2½ teaspoons baking soda
¼ teaspoon salt

½ cup milk
2 cups fresh blueberries
½ cup sugar
½ cup all-purpose flour, sifted
½ teaspoon cinnamon
¼ cup butter

■ Cream the shortening and ½ cup of sugar. Add the egg and mix well. Sift together 2 cups of flour, the baking soda, and salt. Add to the creamed mixture alternately with the milk. Line an 8-inch square pan with waxed paper. Pour the batter into the pan. Sprinkle the blueberries over the batter. Combine the remaining sugar, flour, cinnamon, and butter, and sprinkle over the blueberries. Bake at 375° for 1 hour and 15 minutes.

Recipes

■ ■ ■ ■ ■ ■

BREAKFAST DISHES

APPETIZERS AND SNACKS

BEVERAGES

SOUPS

SALADS

MAIN DISHES

VEGETABLES

BREADS

CONDIMENTS

DESSERTS

Breakfast Dishes
■ ■ ■ ■ ■ ■ ■ ■ ■ ■ ■ ■ ■ ■

SPECIAL SCRAMBLED EGGS

6 eggs
⅓ cup shredded Cheddar
cheese
⅓ cup sour cream

Salt and pepper to taste
8 slices bacon, cooked and
crumbled
2 tablespoons butter

■ Beat the eggs with a fork until well beaten. Blend in the cheese, sour cream, seasonings, and bacon; set aside. In a large skillet over medium heat, heat the butter. Pour in the egg mixture. As it cooks, stir gently with a spoon, continuing until the eggs are set.

CRACKERS AND EGGS
4 servings

2 eggs
1 cup milk
1 4-ounce package saltine
crackers

4 tablespoons butter
Maple syrup

■ In a medium bowl beat the eggs and milk together with a fork or wire whisk until completely blended. Crumble crackers into the egg mixture and stir gently. The batter will be lumpy.

In a skillet over medium heat melt the butter. Pour in the egg and cracker mixture and cook, covered, for approximately 5 minutes. Flip over and cook for another 5 to 7 minutes, until done. Cut into 4 wedges. Serve immediately with warm butter and maple syrup.

CREAMY HAM AND EGGS
4 servings

3 tablespoons butter or
margarine
3 tablespoons all-purpose
flour
2 cups milk
1/2 teaspoon dry mustard

1/8 teaspoon white pepper
1 cup diced cooked ham
4 hard-cooked eggs, quartered
4 slices toasted bread
Parsley (optional)

■ In a heavy saucepan melt the butter over low heat. Add the flour, stirring until smooth. Cook 1 minute, stirring constantly. Gradually add the milk, and stir constantly over medium heat until the mixture is bubbly. Stir in the mustard and pepper. Gently add the ham and eggs. Spoon the ham mixture over the toast and garnish with parsley if desired.

OLD-FASHIONED OATMEAL
6 servings

2½ cups water
⅛ teaspoon salt
2 cups quick-cooking
   oatmeal
2 tablespoons sugar
½ teaspoon ground
   cinnamon

1 5-ounce can sweetened
   condensed milk
3 tablespoons butter
5 tablespoons brown sugar

■ In a large saucepan, bring the water to a boil. Add the salt. Stirring constantly, add the oatmeal, sugar, and cinnamon. Cook for 1 minute. Add the sweetened condensed milk and reheat to boiling. Pour into serving dishes and top with butter and brown sugar.

SAUSAGE GRITS
15 servings

1 pound bulk sausage
3 cups hot cooked grits
2½ cups shredded Cheddar
   cheese
3 tablespoons butter

3 eggs
1½ cups milk
   Pimento strips (optional)
   Parsley (optional)

■ In a heavy skillet cook the sausage until browned. Drain well. Spoon into a lightly greased 13x9x2-inch baking dish.
   Combine the hot grits, cheese and butter, and stir until the cheese and butter melts. In a separate bowl, combine the eggs and milk, and stir into the grits. Pour into the casserole over the sausage. Bake at 350° for 1 hour. Garnish with pimento strips and parsley if desired.

FRIED GRITS
8 servings

4 cups water	½ cup packaged seasoned
1¾ cups milk	bread crumbs
¼ cup butter	1 teaspoon parsley flakes
1½ teaspoons sugar	3 large eggs
1 teaspoon salt	¼ cup milk
2 cups grits	¾ cup oil
1½ cups unsifted all-purpose	
flour	

■ In a large saucepan, combine 2½ cups of water, the milk, butter, sugar, and salt and bring to a boil. In a small bowl, combine the grits and remaining water. Stir the grits mixture into the boiling milk mixture. Cook, stirring constantly, until thick and bubbly. Cover and cook over low heat for 5 minutes. Pour the grits into a greased 9x5-inch loaf pan. Cool to room temperature. Cover tightly and refrigerate until firm, several hours or overnight.

In a large bowl combine the flour, bread crumbs, and parsley. In a separate bowl beat the eggs and milk. Unmold the grits loaf and cut into 16 slices. In a large, deep skillet, heat the oil over high heat. Dip the grit slices in the flour mixture, then the egg mixture, then the flour mixture again. Fry the slices in the hot oil, turning occasionally, until golden brown.

GRANOLA

8 cups old-fashioned oats	½ cup water
1 cup wheat germ	½ cup oil
1 cup sesame seeds	½ cup honey
1 cup unsweetened coconut	1½ teaspoons salt
1 cup raw cashews or	2 teaspoons vanilla extract
almonds	1 cup raisins
½ cup chopped Brazil nuts	

■ In a large baking pan combine the oats, wheat germ, sesame seeds, coconut, and nuts. Mix well. In a bowl combine the water, oil, honey, salt, and vanilla. Add to the dry ingredients and mix well. Bake at 325° for 45 minutes. When cooled, add the raisins.

BUTTERMILK PANCAKES
12 to 15 pancakes

2 cups sifted all-purpose flour
2 tablespoons baking soda
1 teaspoon salt
1 heaping teaspoon sugar
2 eggs
2 cups buttermilk

■ In a large bowl beat all of the ingredients with a spoon. Pour in ¼-cup measures onto a lightly oiled hot griddle.

CORNMEAL-BACON PANCAKES
4 servings

⅓ cup yellow cornmeal
1 cup all-purpose flour
1 teaspoon salt
2 teaspoons baking powder
1 egg
1¼ cups milk
1 tablespoon bacon fat, melted
2 strips bacon, cooked and crumbled
Maple syrup
Butter

■ In a large bowl mix together the cornmeal, flour, salt, and baking powder. In a separate bowl, beat the egg and add the milk and bacon fat. Slowly add the egg mixture to the cornmeal mixture, mixing well. Add the bacon. Pour in ¼ cup measures onto a lightly oiled hot griddle. Serve with maple syrup and butter.

WAFFLES
4 waffles

1 1/2 cups sifted all-purpose
   flour
  1/2 teaspoon salt
  2 teaspoons baking powder

2 eggs, separated
1 cup milk
4 tablespoons melted
  shortening

■ Sift the flour, salt and baking powder together. In a large bowl beat the egg yolks and add the milk and shortening. Add the flour mixture and beat with a rotary mixer until smooth. Beat the egg whites until stiff and fold into the batter. Bake in a hot waffle iron.

BLUEBERRY CORN MUFFINS
6 muffins

3/4 cup yellow cornmeal
 1 cup all-purpose flour
1/2 teaspoon salt
 2 teaspoons baking powder
 1 egg plus 1 egg white

1/2 cup buttermilk
1/2 cup melted butter
1 1/2 cups fresh or frozen
  blueberries

■ Combine the dry ingredients, then add the eggs, buttermilk, and melted butter. Stir until just blended. Fold in the blueberries and turn into 6 greased muffin cups, filling almost completely. Bake at 400° for 20 to 25 minutes.

FUDGE MUFFINS
24 muffins

4 ounces semi-sweet
  chocolate
1 cup melted margarine
1 cup sugar
1/2 teaspoon salt

1 cup all-purpose flour
4 eggs
1 teaspoon vanilla extract
2 cups chopped walnuts

■ In a saucepan melt the chocolate in the melted margarine. Beat in the sugar, salt and flour. Add the eggs, one at a time. Add the vanilla and chopped walnuts. Pour into a greased 24-cup muffin pan and bake at 325° for 25 minutes.

MOLASSES MUFFINS
18 muffins

1 cup shortening
⅔ cup sugar
1 cup molasses
3 eggs
1 cup buttermilk
1 teaspoon baking soda
1 teaspoon baking powder

½ teaspoon cloves
½ teaspoon ginger
½ teaspoon allspice
½ teaspoon nutmeg
½ teaspoon cinnamon
All-purpose flour

■ Cream the shortening and add the sugar, molasses, and eggs. Beat well. Add the remaining ingredients. Add flour until the batter is stiff. Pour into greased muffin cups and bake at 350° until done.

RAISIN GRITS MUFFINS
16 muffins

¼ cup butter
2½ cups all-purpose flour
1½ cups quick-cooking grits
⅓ cup sugar
2½ tablespoons baking
   powder
1 teaspoon ground
   cinnamon

¾ teaspoon salt
1½ cups milk
2 large eggs
2 teaspoons vanilla extract
¾ cup raisins
2 tablespoons cinnamon-
   sugar mixture

■ In a small saucepan melt the butter over low heat and set aside to cool. In a large bowl, mix the flour, grits, sugar, baking powder, cinnamon, and salt. Set aside.

Beat the milk, then the eggs, and vanilla into the melted butter until just blended. Stir into the flour mixture just until moistened. Gently fold in the raisins. Spoon the batter into 16 greased muffin cups. Sprinkle with cinnamon sugar. Bake at 400° for 20 minutes or until a wooden toothpick inserted in the center comes out clean. Serve warm.

Spicy Peach Muffins
18 to 24 muffins

4½ cups all-purpose flour
1 teaspoon salt
4½ teaspoons baking powder
¾ cup sugar
¾ cup packed brown sugar

½ teaspoon nutmeg
1 teaspoon cinnamon
2 eggs
¾ cup vegetable oil
1¼ cups milk
2 peaches, peeled and diced

■ Combine the flour, salt, baking powder, sugar, brown sugar, and spices. Slowly add the eggs, oil, and milk, stirring until just blended. Stir in the diced peaches. Fill greased muffin tins ⅞ full. Bake at 400° for 25 to 30 minutes.

Dried Fruit Sour Cream Coffee Cake
16 servings

¾ cup margarine
1½ cups sugar
2 eggs
1 teaspoon vanilla extract
2 teaspoons baking powder
½ teaspoon baking soda
½ teaspoon salt
2¼ cups all-purpose flour
1 cup (½ pint) sour cream

¼ cup chopped walnuts
¼ cup chopped dried dates
¼ cup chopped prunes
¼ cup chopped dried apricots
½ teaspoon cinnamon
2 tablespoons sugar

■ In a large bowl cream together the margarine and 1½ cups of sugar. Add the eggs and beat until light. Mix in the vanilla, baking powder, baking soda, salt, and half the flour. Add the sour cream and beat until smooth. Beat in the remaining flour. Stir in the walnuts and fruits. Spread the batter into a greased and floured 10-inch tube pan. Combine the cinnamon and 2 tablespoons of sugar and sprinkle over the batter. Bake at 350° for 45 minutes.

APPLE COFFEE CAKE
6 to 8 servings

1 20-ounce can apple pie
  filling
2 teaspoons ground
  cinnamon
3 cups all-purpose flour
1 cup sugar
1½ cups milk
½ cup butter, softened

3 teaspoons baking powder
1 teaspoon salt
3 eggs
¼ cup packed brown sugar
¼ cup chopped nuts
2 tablespoons butter, melted

■ Combine the pie filling and cinnamon, and set aside. In a large bowl combine the flour, sugar, milk, ½ cup of butter, baking powder, salt, and eggs. Beat at medium speed of an electric mixer for 30 seconds, then beat at medium speed for 2 minutes. Pour half of the batter into a greased 9x13-inch pan. Spoon half of the pie filling over the batter. Repeat with the remaining batter and pie filling. Sprinkle the brown sugar and nuts over the pie filling and drizzle with melted butter. Bake at 350° for 35 to 40 minutes or until a wooden toothpick inserted in the center comes out clean.

Nutmeg Coffee Cake
12 servings

2¼ cups light brown sugar,
  firmly packed
3 cups sifted all-purpose
  flour
¾ cup butter
1 cup (½ pint) sour cream

1½ teaspoons baking soda
2 eggs
1 teaspoon ground nutmeg
¾ cup chopped walnuts

■ In a large bowl combine the brown sugar and flour, and cut in the butter with a pastry blender or 2 knives until the mixture resembles coarse crumbs. Reserve ¾ cup of the butter mixture. Combine the sour cream and baking soda, and stir into the remaining crumbs with the eggs and nutmeg. Pour into a greased and floured 9x3x1-inch baking pan and sprinkle with the nuts and reserved crumb mixture. Bake at 350° for 40 minutes or until a wooden toothpick inserted in the center comes out clean.

Marmalade Biscuits
18 biscuits

2 cups all-purpose flour
1⅓ tablespoons baking
  powder
½ teaspoon salt
¼ cup plus 1 tablespoon
  shortening

1 egg, slightly beaten
⅓ cup milk
⅓ cup orange marmalade

■ Mix together the flour, baking powder, and salt. Cut in the shortening until the mixture resembles coarse meal. Combine the egg, milk, and marmalade. Add to the flour mixture, stirring until moistened. Turn the dough onto a lightly floured surface. Knead lightly 8 or 10 times. Roll the dough ½-inch thick and cut with a 2-inch biscuit cutter. Place the biscuits on an ungreased baking sheet. Bake at 450° for 8 to 10 minutes or until golden brown. Serve hot with additional marmalade, if desired.

Appetizers and Snacks

■■■■■■■■■■■■■■■■■■■

BEEF JERKY
80 pieces

1 1- to 1½-pound flank steak
1 teaspoon seasoned salt
1 teaspoon liquid smoke
⅓ teaspoon pepper
1 teaspoon onion powder

¼ cup soy sauce
⅓ teaspoon garlic powder
1 teaspoon MSG
¼ cup Worcestershire sauce

■ Trim all the fat from the steak and cut with the grain into ⅛-inch slices. Arrange the steak slices in a shallow glass dish. In a separate bowl combine the remaining ingredients. Pour over the steak slices and mix well. Marinate overnight.

Drain the steak well and arrange the slices in a single layer on an oven rack. Place foil beneath the rack to catch the drippings. Turn the oven to the lowest possible temperature and bake, leaving the door ajar, for 6 to 12 hours, or until the slices are completely dry.

TASTY BLACK-EYED PEA DIP
10 to 12 servings

½ pound dried black beans	1 cup tomato juice
2 cups water	½ cup chopped onion
1¼ teaspoons salt	⅛ teaspoon garlic powder
⅓ cup diced lean ham	4 ounces cheese spread
½ teaspoon red food	(½ an 8-ounce jar)
coloring	¼ teaspoon hot pepper sauce
1 4-ounce can green chilies	

■ Wash the peas and cover with water; soak overnight. Drain the peas and cover with water in a heavy saucepan; bring to a boil. Lower the temperature; cover and simmer for 30 minutes. Add the salt and ham and simmer for 25 to 30 minutes longer. Add the red food coloring. Drain the peas, reserving the liquid.

Drain and chop the chilies, reserving 2 tablespoons of liquid. Place the peas, chilies, reserved juice from the chilies, tomato juice, onion and garlic powder in a blender container; blend to make a puree. (If a blender is not available, put the mixture through a food mill.) Add a small amount of the liquid reserved from the peas, if needed, to obtain the desired consistency. Spoon the mixture into the top of a double boiler; add the cheese spread and pepper sauce. Cook over medium heat until the cheese melts. Serve warm with crackers or corn chips.

PEPPERY CHEESE TWISTS
2 dozen

1½ cups all-purpose flour	¼ teaspoon black pepper
1½ teaspoons baking powder	¼ cup unsalted butter,
½ teaspoon salt	cut into pieces
¼ teaspoon dry mustard	1 cup shredded Monterey
¼ teaspoon ground hot red	Jack cheese
pepper	5 tablespoons cold water

■ In a medium bowl combine the flour, baking powder, salt, mustard, red and black pepper, and stir to mix well.

Cut in the butter with a pastry blender or two knives until the mixture resembles coarse meal. Stir in the cheese. Sprinkle the water over the top, and toss with a fork until moistened. Press together to form a ball. Turn out onto a lightly floured surface. Cut the dough in half. Roll each half into a 12x6-inch rectangle. Cut lengthwise into ½-inch strips. Twist slightly and place on 2 greased cookie sheets. Bake at 350° for 15 to 18 minutes or until browned.

PARTY MIX
16 cups

1 1-ounce envelope ranch salad dressing mix
2 tablespoons dried whole dillweed
6 cups corn and rice cereal
1 10-ounce package oyster crackers
1 6.5-ounce package small pretzels
¾ cup oil

■ In a large bowl combine the salad dressing mix and the dillweed. Add the cereal, oyster crackers, and pretzels, tossing well. Drizzle the oil over the mixture and stir to combine. Place the mixture in a large paper bag and fold to close. Let stand for 2 hours, shaking the bag occasionally. Store the party mix in an airtight container.

HOT-AS-FIRE PEANUTS

2 egg whites
2 to 3 tablespoons bottled red pepper sauce
1 tablespoon Worcestershire sauce
2 pounds unsalted peanuts

■ In a large bowl beat the egg whites until soft peaks form. Fold in the red pepper sauce and Worcestershire sauce. Add the peanuts and toss until evenly coated. Spread the peanuts into two greased 15x10x1-inch jelly-roll pans and bake at 250° for 45 minutes, stirring every 15 minutes.

These may be stored in an airtight container up to one month; they get hotter as they age.

Ham balls
60 balls

1 pound ground beef
1 pound ground ham
2 eggs
1½ cups graham cracker
  crumbs

1 cup packed light brown
  sugar
1 teaspoon prepared mustard
½ cup water
½ cup vinegar

■ In a large bowl mix together the beef, ham, eggs, and cracker crumbs until well blended. Shape into balls and place on a large, rimmed baking sheet. In a separate bowl, stir together the remaining ingredients until well blended. Pour over the ham balls. Bake at 350° for 1½ hours.

Mock chicken livers
30 servings

1 pound sliced bacon

½ to 1 pound pitted dates

■ Cut the bacon slices into thirds. Wrap each bacon portion around a date and secure with a toothpick. Place on a rack in a baking pan and bake at 350° until the bacon is crisp. Drain on paper towels and serve hot.

Garden fresh salsa

2 slices bacon
2 medium onions, chopped
4 cups chopped tomatoes
1 small chile pepper, chopped

1 clove garlic, crushed
1 teaspoon sugar
½ teaspoon cumin seeds,
  crushed
1 tablespoon lemon juice

■ In a large Dutch oven cook the bacon until crisp. Remove the bacon and reserve 2 tablespoons of drippings. Crumble the bacon and set aside.

Sauté the onion in the tomatoes and simmer for 15 minutes. Add the remaining ingredients and stir to combine.

This is good served in hollowed green or yellow peppers, with tortilla chips.

Beverages

■ ■ ■ ■ ■ ■ ■ ■ ■

Tennessee Boiled Custard

8 servings

    1 cup sugar, divided
    4 cups milk, divided
    3 eggs, well beaten
2½ tablespoons all-purpose
    flour

⅛ teaspoon baking soda
1 teaspoon vanilla extract

■ In the top of a double boiler combine ½ cup of sugar and 3 cups of milk and heat over boiling water. In a medium bowl combine the eggs, remaining sugar, flour, soda, and remaining milk. Blend well and pour through a strainer into the hot milk mixture, stirring constantly. Cook over boiling water, stirring frequently for 10 to 13 minutes or until the mixture will coat a metal spoon. Stir in the vanilla extract. Cool.

HOT COCOA-COFFEE MIX
6½ cups dry mix

2 cups non-dairy coffee
   creamer
1½ cups hot cocoa mix
1½ cups instant coffee
   granules

1½ cups sugar
1 teaspoon ground
   cinnamon
½ teaspoon ground nutmeg

■ Combine all of the ingredients and mix well. Store in an airtight container.

To make 1 serving, place 2 tablespoons plus 1 teaspoon of mix in a cup and add 1 cup of boiling water. Stir until blended.

INSTANT SPICED TEA
5 cups dry mix

2 cups orange-flavored
   instant breakfast drink
¾ cup instant tea with lemon
   and sugar

¼ teaspoon ground cinnamon
2 cups sugar
¼ teaspoon ground cloves

■ Combine all of the ingredients and mix well. Store in an airtight container.

To make 1 serving place 3 teaspoons of tea mix in a mug and add 1 cup of boiling water. Stir until blended.

BUTTERY MULLED CIDER
6 servings

½ cup brown sugar
   Juice from 1 orange
   Juice from 1 lemon
½ gallon apple cider

4 whole cloves
2 cinnamon sticks
1 teaspoon whole allspice
3 tablespoons butter

■ In a large saucepan heat the sugar and juices until syrupy. Add the cider, cloves, cinnamon sticks, and allspice, and simmer covered for 1 hour. Strain to remove the spices. Pour into mugs and float ½ tablespoon of butter on top of each.

HOT SPICED FRUIT TEA
3 quarts

1 teaspoon whole cloves
1 2-inch stick cinnamon
3 quarts boiling water
3 1-quart tea bags

1 to 1½ cups sugar
1 cup orange juice
¼ cup plus 2 tablespoons
   lemon juice

■ Tie the cloves and cinnamon in a cheesecloth and set aside. Pour the boiling water over the tea bags and cover. Steep for 5 minutes. Discard the bags. In a large Dutch oven combine the tea, sugar, juices, and spice bag and bring to a boil. Reduce the heat, and simmer for 15 to 20 minutes. Discard the spice bag.

COLD WEATHER CRANBERRY PUNCH
10 to 12 servings

2 cups water
1 cup sugar
4 cinnamon sticks
1 6-ounce can frozen orange
   juice concentrate

1 6-ounce can frozen
   lemonade concentrate
1 quart cranberry juice

■ Boil the water, sugar, and cinnamon for 10 minutes. Combine the orange juice, lemonade, and cranberry juice and add to the syrup.

To make 1 serving, add ¾ cup of juice mixture to 1 cup of water and heat through.

HOT SPICED LEMONADE
4 servings

3 cups water
⅔ cup packed light brown
  sugar
½ cup lemon juice from
  concentrate

8 whole cloves
2 cinnamon sticks
  Cinnamon sticks for
  garnish (optional)

■ In a medium saucepan combine all of the ingredients except the garnish. Simmer uncovered for 20 minutes. Remove the spices. Serve in hot mugs with cinnamon sticks, if desired.

ALMOND TEA
3 quarts

2 tablespoons lemon-
  flavored ice tea mix
2 cups hot water
1½ cups sugar
10 cups water, divided

1 12-ounce can frozen
  lemonade concentrate
1 tablespoon almond extract
2 teaspoons vanilla extract

■ Dissolve the iced tea mix in the hot water and set aside. In a Dutch oven combine the sugar and 2 cups of water. Bring to a boil, and boil for 5 minutes. Add the tea mixture, remaining water, and remaining ingredients to the sugar syrup. Heat thoroughly.

TEA PUNCH
1 gallon

7 tea bags
2 cups sugar
2 6-ounce cans frozen orange
  juice concentrate

2 6-ounce cans frozen
  lemonade concentrate
Water to finish 1 gallon
Sprigs of fresh mint

■ Brew the tea according to the package directions. In a gallon container combine the remaining ingredients, and add the tea.

Other juices such as peach, pear, pineapple, and apricot may be added, but the amount of sugar should be reduced when sweetened juices are used.

WHITE GRAPE JUICE TEA
1 gallon

1 gallon water
3 family-sized tea bags
2 to 2½ cups sugar

¾ cup white grape juice
1 .32-ounce envelope unsweetened lemonade-flavored drink mix

■ Bring the water to a boil; pour over the tea bags. Cover, and steep for 5 minutes. Discard the tea bags and add the remaining ingredients, stir well. Serve chilled.

OLD-FASHIONED LEMONADE
6 servings

6 or 7 lemons
½ to ¾ cup sugar

4 cups cold water
Ice cubes

■ Wash the lemons and thinly slice two. In a 6-cup pitcher combine the sliced lemons and desired amount of sugar. Press the lemons with a potato masher or wooden spoon to release the juice. Squeeze enough of the remaining lemons to make ⅔ cup of juice. Add to the lemons in the pitcher, along with the cold water. Stir to combine.

Serve in chilled glasses over ice cubes.

COCA COLA PUNCH
25 servings

Juice of 12 lemons
3 cups sugar

5 pints water
6 16-ounce Coca Colas

■ Combine the lemon juice, sugar, and water. Refrigerate overnight. When ready to serve, add the Coca Colas and ice.

CHRISTMAS PARTY PUNCH
50 servings

1 12-ounce can frozen orange
juice concentrate
1 6-ounce can frozen
lemonade concentrate

2½ cups pineapple juice
6 pints cranberry juice
cocktail

■ Add water to the frozen concentrates as directed on the cans. Add the pineapple juice and the cranberry juice and mix well. Serve in a punch bowl over ice.

FRUIT MEDLEY PUNCH
25 servings

2 10-ounce packages frozen
strawberries in syrup
3 cups apricot nectar
3 cups cold water
1 6-ounce can frozen orange
juice concentrate, thawed

1 cup lemon juice from
concentrate
1 cup sugar
1 32-ounce bottle ginger ale,
chilled

■ In a blender puree the partially thawed strawberries well. In a punch bowl combine the pureed strawberries, apricot nectar, water, juices, and sugar. Stir until the sugar dissolves. Slowly pour in the ginger ale.

Soups

■ ■ ■ ■ ■

BROCCOLI-CHEESE SOUP

1 cup water
1 chicken bouillon cube
1 10-ounce package frozen
  broccoli
1 medium carrot, grated
2 tablespoons butter
3 tablespoons all-purpose
  flour
2 cups milk

1 pound processed American
  cheese, cubed
1 10¾-ounce can cream of
  chicken soup
1 tablespoon minced onion
  flakes
1 tablespoon Worcestershire
  sauce
Salt and pepper to taste

■ Bring the water and bouillon cube to a boil. Add the
broccoli and carrot, and cook according to package directions. Remove from heat and do not drain. In a separate
saucepan make a white sauce by melting the butter and
slowly stirring in the flour. Continue stirring while gradually adding the milk. Stir in the cheese, chicken soup,
onion, Worcestershire sauce, salt and pepper. Add the broccoli and carrot mixture to the white sauce mixture and
cook over low heat until thickened.

COUNTRY CHICKEN SOUP
6 to 8 servings

1 carrot, chopped
¾ cup chopped celery
1 sweet green pepper,
  chopped
1 onion, chopped
¾ cup cubed cooked chicken
1 apple, peeled and cubed
4 tablespoons butter

⅓ cup all-purpose flour
2 whole cloves
1 sprig parsley
4 cups chicken broth
1 cup canned or fresh
  tomatoes
Salt to taste
2½ to 3 cups milk

■ Sauté the carrot, celery, green pepper and onion lightly in butter, stirring often. Add the chicken and remaining ingredients, except the milk. Simmer covered for 50 minutes. Add the milk and bring to a boil.

CREAM OF CHICKEN SOUP
6 servings

2 tablespoons butter
3 tablespoons all-purpose
  flour
7 cups chicken broth
  Carcass of a chicken

1 onion, finely chopped
1 carrot, finely chopped
1 stalk celery, finely chopped
2 egg yolks
½ cup light cream

■ In a large saucepan heat the butter. Add the flour and stir in the chicken broth with a wire whisk. Add the chicken carcass, onion, carrot, and celery and simmer for 1 hour. Remove the carcass, strain the soup and return to a clean saucepan. Combine the egg yolks and cream and add to the soup. Heat through, but do not boil or the egg yolks will curdle.

OLD-FASHIONED POTATO-NOODLE SOUP
6 servings

1 quart water	2 eggs, lightly beaten
1 teaspoon salt	Milk
3 medium sized potatoes, sliced	½ cup salted butter
2 cups all-purpose flour	1 cup milk
	Onion, chopped

■ In a 6 quart pot bring the water and ½ teaspoon of salt to a boil, then add the potatoes and cook until done. With a potato masher or fork, mash them in the water.

While the potatoes are cooking, sift the flour and ½ teaspoon salt together in a medium size mixing bowl. In a 1-cup measuring cup, lightly beat the eggs and finish filling the cup with milk. Add the milk mixture to the flour mixture, making a very soft dough.

Bring the potato water to boiling. Add ½ cup of butter and 1 cup of milk and bring to a simmering boil. Keep simmering. Dip a teaspoon into the hot soup and then dip up about ½ teaspoon of dough on tip of spoon. Drop into the simmering soup, stir, and keep up the process until all of the dough has been used. Stir continuously. If it seems a little thick, add milk. Cover and cook about 20 minutes. Serve with chopped onions sprinkled on top.

FRESH TOMATO SOUP
6 cups

¼ cup butter	1 teaspoon salt
½ cup chopped onion	½ teaspoon dried whole
¼ cup all-purpose flour	thyme
1 cup water	¼ teaspoon pepper
6 medium tomatoes, peeled	1 bay leaf
and coarsely chopped	Lemon slices for garnish
1 tablespoon minced fresh	(optional)
parsley	Bay leaves for garnish
1 tablespoon sugar	(optional)

■ In a large Dutch oven melt the butter and then sauté onion until tender. Reduce the heat to low and then add the flour, stirring until smooth. Cook for 1 minute, stirring constantly. Gradually add the water and cook over medium heat, stirring constantly, until thickened and bubbly. Add the remaining ingredients except the garnishes and bring to a boil, then cover and reduce heat, simmering for 30 minutes. Remove and discard the bay leaf. Spoon one-third of the tomato mixture into the bowl of an electric blender and process until smooth. Repeat procedure with remaining tomato mixture. Garnish with the lemon slices and additional bay leaves, if desired.

CREAMY BLACK-EYED PEA SOUP
2½ quarts

1 cup dried black-eyed peas	¼ teaspoon pepper
2 quarts water	1 cup diced cooked carrot
1 clove garlic, minced	1 quart milk
1 large onion, sliced	¾ pound bulk pork sausage
½ bay leaf	Chopped parsley
2 teaspoons salt	

■ Wash the peas and soak in water for 2 hours. Add the garlic, onion, and bay leaf, then simmer for 1½ hours or until the peas are tender. Add salt and pepper. Mash the peas with a potato masher, then add the carrots and milk.

Shape the sausage into tiny balls and fry slowly until done. Sprinkle the soup with parsley and add the sausage balls.

Ham and bean soup
1 gallon

1 pound dried Great Northern beans	2 cups water
6 cups water	4 medium potatoes, peeled and quartered
1½ pounds ham or hamhock, cooked and cubed	3 carrots, scraped and cut into ½ inch slices
2 teaspoons salt	1 medium onion, finely chopped
3 cloves garlic, minced	

■ Sort and wash the beans. Place in a Dutch oven and cover with water 2 inches above the beans. Soak overnight and then drain. In the Dutch oven combine the beans, 6 cups of water, ham, salt, and garlic and bring to a boil. Cover, reduce heat and simmer 1½ hours. Then add 2 cups water and vegetables to beans. Cover and simmer about 30 minutes or until vegetables are tender.

Squash soup
6 servings

6 to 8 green onions, greens discarded	1 cup heavy cream
4 tablespoons butter	Salt to taste
2 pounds summer squash, diced	White pepper to taste
4 cups chicken stock or broth	6 tablespoons sour cream
	Chopped chives

■ In a large saucepan sauté the onions in butter until softened, then stir in the squash. Add the chicken broth, bring to a boil and simmer, covered, for ½ hour or until the vegetables are soft. Puree in a blender and return to the pan. Stir in the cream, salt, and pepper and reheat. Garnish each serving with one tablespoon of sour cream and a sprinkle of chives.

GARDEN VEGETABLE SOUP
11 cups

2 16-ounce cans whole
 tomatoes, undrained and
 chopped
1 quart water
½ pound okra, sliced
½ pound green beans, cut
 into 1-inch pieces
1 large onion, chopped
2 stalks celery, chopped
2 carrots, thinly sliced

1½ cups cabbage, coarsely
 chopped
1¼ teaspoons salt
 ½ teaspoon dried parsley
 flakes
Dash of pepper
Dash of onion powder
Dash of garlic powder

■ In a large Dutch oven, combine all of the ingredients.
Cover and simmer for 1 hour and 20 minutes, stirring occasionally.

CREAMY CORN CHOWDER

¼ pound bacon, diced
2 tablespoons bacon
 drippings
1 cup chopped onion
1 green pepper, chopped
2½ cups chicken broth
2 cups diced potatoes
1 15-ounce can creamed
 corn

1 teaspoon paprika
½ teaspoon pepper
¼ teaspoon sage
2 cups milk or half and half
 Salt to taste

■ In a Dutch oven brown the bacon. Drain, reserving 2 tablepoons of drippings. Sauté the onion and green pepper in
the bacon drippings until soft. Add the chicken broth and
diced potatoes. Bring to a boil and simmer until the potatoes are cooked. Add the corn, seasonings, bacon and
milk. Heat through.

Farm Style Beef Stew
6 to 8 servings

2 tablespoons shortening
3 pounds stewing beef, cubed
2 large onions, sliced
1 20-ounce can tomatoes
2 cloves garlic, pressed
1 cup celery, sliced
1/4 cup chopped parsley
1 bay leaf
1/2 tablespoon ground thyme

1 tablespoon salt
1/2 teaspoon freshly ground
   pepper
2 1/2 cups water
12 small carrots, sliced
1 cup English peas
12 small white onions
6 potatoes, quartered
1/2 cup flour
3/4 cup cold water

■ Melt the shortening in a 6-quart pot and brown meat, then add the next 10 ingredients. Bring to a boil, reduce heat, cover and simmer 2 hours. Add the next 4 ingredients and simmer, covered, for 1 hour. Blend the flour with cold water and stir into the stew to thicken.

Church Stew
8 gallons

10 pounds chuck roast
10 pounds pork roast
12 pounds stewing hens
2 pounds dry white beans,
   soaked overnight
5 pounds onions, sliced
1 gallon fresh cut corn

1/2 cup salt
1/4 cup black pepper
2 tablespoons cayenne pepper
3 gallons fresh tomatoes,
   peeled

■ Salt the meats and cook until tender in a moderate amount of water. When cool, skin and bone the hens, cut all meat into larger than bite sized pieces, and return it to the broth. In an outdoor cooking pot, or the equivalent, cook the beans and onions until tender but firm in just enough water to cover. Add corn, salt and peppers. Stir continually to keep the corn from sticking. Cook for 30 minutes. Add the tomatoes and cook for 30 more minutes. Add the meat and broth to the cooked vegetable mixture. The consistency should be rather thick.

OYSTER STEW

1 pint oysters and liquid
½ cup melted butter
1 cup light cream, heated
3 cups milk, scalded

½ teaspoon salt
½ teaspoon paprika
Pepper to taste

■ Combine the oysters, liquid, and butter, and heat until the edges of the oysters curl. Add the warm cream and milk. Bring to nearly boiling and add the seasonings. Serve at once.

FANTASTIC FISH CHOWDER
8 to 12 servings

¼ cup oil
2 medium onions, chopped
4 carrots, thinly sliced
¼ cup minced parsley
4 medium potatoes, diced
3 cloves garlic, minced
½ teaspoon pepper

1 teaspoon salt
2 8-ounce cans tomato
  sauce
4 cups hot water
2 pounds fish fillets
2 7-ounce cans whole baby
  clams

■ In a 5-quart Dutch oven heat the oil and sauté the onions, carrots, parsley, potatoes, and garlic until soft. Add the pepper, salt, tomato sauce, and hot water. Bring to a boil. Cut the fish fillets into 1-inch pieces. Add the fish and the clams with their liquid. Cover and reduce the heat. Simmer for about 30 minutes.

CHICKEN-OKRA GUMBO
6 servings

¼ cup butter	6 tomatoes, peeled, seeded
1 4-pound chicken, cut up	and chopped
1 large onion, chopped	½ pound okra, sliced
¼ cup chopped celery	¼ cup chopped parsley
¼ cup chopped green pepper	6 cups hot water
1 cup chopped smoked	1½ teaspoons red pepper
sausage	sauce
	Salt to taste
	Cooked rice

■ In a large saucepan over medium heat melt the butter
and brown the chicken pieces. Remove the chicken, lower
the heat, and sauté the onions, celery, pepper, and sausage
for about 5 minutes. Add the tomatoes, okra, and parsley.
Cook over medium heat, stirring constantly, until the okra
is golden. Stir in the hot water, red pepper sauce, salt, and
chicken pieces. Simmer covered for 1 hour. Serve over
cooked rice.

FLUFFY PAPRIKA DUMPLINGS
8 servings

2 cups all-purpose flour	2 tablespoons shortening
3 teaspoons baking powder	1 cup milk
1 teaspoon salt	Chicken broth or stew
¼ teaspoon paprika	Parsley for garnish

■ Sift the flour, baking powder, salt, and paprika into a
bowl. Cut in the shortening until the mixture is crumbly.
Stir in the milk until moist. The dough will be soft. Drop
the batter into the boiling broth in 8 mounds. Reduce the
heat to simmer. Cover and simmer for 20 minutes. Do not
peek, or they will not be fluffy and light.
    To serve, sprinkle with paprika and garnish with parsley.

Salads

■ ■ ■ ■ ■ ■

BLUEBERRY FRUIT SALAD

1 cup fresh blueberries
1 small banana, sliced
1 cup sliced strawberries
1 cup halved seedless grapes
2 cups cubed cantaloupe

4 tablespoons orange juice,
  divided
¼ cup mayonnaise
¼ cup plain yogurt
 1 tablespoon honey
¼ teaspoon ground ginger

■ In a bowl combine the fruits and 2 tablespoons of the orange juice and toss gently. In a separate bowl combine the remaining ingredients and chill thoroughly before serving over the fruit.

CHERRY COLA SALAD

1 21-ounce can pie cherries
1 cup sugar
2 3-ounce packages cherry
  gelatin

½ cup boiling water
1 16-ounce bottle cola
1 cup chopped nuts

■ Combine the cherries and sugar in a saucepan and bring to a boil. Strain the juice and pour over the gelatin. Add the boiling water to dissolve the gelatin, then add the cola. Chill until the mixture begins to thicken, then add the cherries and nuts. Pour into molds and chill until set.

GEORGE WASHINGTON SALAD

2 3-ounce packages cherry
  gelatin
2 cups boiling water
1 16-ounce can crushed
  pineapple
1 21-ounce can cherry pie
  filling

1 8-ounce package cream
  cheese
1 pint sour cream
½ cup confectioners' sugar
1 teaspoon vanilla extract
½ cup chopped nuts

■ Dissolve the gelatin in boiling water. Add the pineapple and pie filling. Chill until set. Combine the remaining ingredients except the nuts and spread over the gelatin. Sprinkle with nuts.

MINCEMEAT SALAD
12 to 14 servings

1 ¼-ounce envelope
  unflavored gelatin
¼ cup cold water
1 6-ounce package cherry
  gelatin
3½ cups boiling water
1 20½-ounce jar brandy-
  flavored mincemeat

1 8-ounce can crushed
  pineapple, drained
1 small apple, unpeeled and
  finely chopped
1 cup chopped pecans or
  walnuts

■ Soften the gelatin in cold water and set aside. Dissolve the cherry gelatin in the boiling water. Add the unflavored gelatin and stir until dissolved. Chill until the mixture starts to thicken. Stir in the mincemeat, pineapple, apple, and nuts. Pour into a lightly-oiled mold. Chill until firm.

ORANGE SHERBET SALAD
6 servings

1 6-ounce package orange gelatin
2 cups boiling water
1 pint orange sherbet
1 11-ounce can mandarin oranges

2 bananas, sliced
1 8-ounce can crushed pineapple

■ Dissolve the gelatin in the boiling water. Add the sherbet and stir until dissolved. Add the remaining ingredients. Chill until firm.

PEPPERMINT STICK SALAD
8 to 10 servings

1 3-ounce package lime gelatin
1 cup hot water
¾ cup pineapple juice
½ pint heavy cream, whipped

1 16-ounce can crushed pineapple
¾ cup pecans, chopped
6 sticks peppermint candy, crushed

■ Dissolve the gelatin in hot water. Add the pineapple juice, chill until firm, then beat until fluffy. Fold in the whipped cream. Add the pineapple, nuts, and half of the crushed candy. Chill until ready to serve. Sprinkle the remaining crushed candy over the salad.

SPICED PEACH SALAD

6 servings

1 16-ounce can sliced
  peaches
¼ cup vinegar
½ cup sugar
12 whole cloves

⅛ teaspoon cinnamon
1 3-ounce package orange
  gelatin
¾ cup cold water

■ Drain the peaches, reserving 1 cup of syrup. Chop the peaches coarsely. Bring the syrup, vinegar, sugar, and spices to a boil and simmer for 10 minutes. Strain the syrup and discard the cloves. Dissolve the gelatin in the hot syrup. Add the cold water and peaches. Chill until slightly thickened. Pour into a mold and chill until set.

WALDORF SALAD

3 apples, cored
1 tablespoon lemon juice
¾ cup chopped walnuts

⅓ cup chopped celery
½ cup mayonnaise
Lettuce leaves

■ Cut a few slices of apples for garnish and dice the remaining apples. Coat the apples with lemon juice. Toss the apples with the walnuts, celery, and mayonnaise. Serve on lettuce leaves.

Sour Cream Potato Salad
8 to 10 servings

6 to 8 medium potatoes	2 tablespoons vinegar
2 tablespoons sweet pickle relish	1 tablespoon prepared mustard
2 tablespoons finely chopped onion	1 teaspoon salt
2 tablespoons chopped fresh parsley	Pepper to taste
	1/2 pint sour cream
1 2-ounce jar chopped pimento, drained	1 1/2 cups chopped celery
	2 hard-cooked eggs, chopped

■ Cook the potatoes in boiling water for 15 to 20 minutes or until tender. Drain and cool. Peel the potatoes, then cut into 1/2-inch cubes; set aside.

In a large bowl combine the next 8 ingredients and fold in the sour cream. Add the potatoes, celery, and eggs; toss gently. Chill at least 1 hour.

Congealed Coleslaw Salad
6 to 8 servings

1 package lemon gelatin	1/4 cup sliced radishes
1 cup boiling water	1/2 cup diced celery
1/2 cup mayonnaise	2 to 4 tablespoons diced green pepper
1/2 cup cold water	1 tablespoon diced onion
2 tablespoons vinegar	
1/4 teaspoon salt	
1 1/2 cups shredded cabbage	

■ Dissolve the gelatin in boiling water. Blend in the mayonnaise, cold water, vinegar, and salt. Chill the mixture until partially set, then beat until fluffy. Add the cabbage, radish slices, celery, green pepper, and onion. Pour into a 1-quart mold. Chill until firm.

HAM COLESLAW
2 servings

1 cup shredded cabbage
½ cup cubed cooked ham
2 tablespoons chopped green
  pepper
1 tablespoon chopped
  pimento, drained
2 tablespoons oil

1 tablespoon vinegar
½ teaspoon sugar
½ teaspoon celery seed
¼ teaspoon salt
¼ teaspoon dry mustard
⅛ teaspoon pepper
⅛ teaspoon paprika

■ In a large serving bowl, combine the first 4 ingredients and mix well. In a separate bowl, combine the remaining ingredients and mix well. Pour over the cabbage mixture and toss gently. Serve immediately.

SWEET AND SOUR COLESLAW
10 servings

1 medium cabbage, shredded
1 large white onion, thinly
  sliced
1 tablespoon salt
1 cup sugar

1 cup white vinegar
¾ cup oil
2 teaspoons celery seed
2 teaspoons mustard seed

■ In a large bowl, layer half of the cabbage, the onion, and the remaining cabbage. Combine the salt and sugar, and sprinkle over the cabbage.

In a saucepan bring the remaining ingredients to a boil. Pour evenly over the cabbage, and do not stir. Cover and refrigerate overnight. Before serving, toss well and drain.

COLESLAW DRESSING

⅓ cup cider vinegar
⅓ cup oil
¼ cup sugar

1 teaspoon salt
¼ teaspoon celery seed
2 sprigs parsley, minced

■ Stir all of the ingredients together until well blended. Pour over slaw and serve at once.

CUCUMBER DRESSING
1 pint

1 cup mayonnaise	*1 teaspoon chopped parsley*
1 cup chopped cucumber	*½ teaspoon salt*
2 teaspoons chopped chives	*½ teaspoon dill weed*

■ Combine all ingredients and chill. This dressing is delicious when served over green salads.

HONEY-FRENCH DRESSING
1½ cups

1 cup oil	*½ teaspoon dry mustard*
¼ cup vinegar	*½ teaspoon paprika*
¼ cup lemon juice	*⅓ cup honey*
1 teaspoon salt	

■ Beat all of the ingredients together, and store in the refrigerator. Shake well before serving.

POPPY SEED DRESSING
1 cup

¾ cup sugar	*1 cup oil*
1 teaspoon salt	*1½ tablespoons onion juice*
1 teaspoon dry mustard	*2 tablespoons poppy seeds*
3 tablespoons vinegar	

■ Combine the dry ingredients and add the vinegar. Mix well. Add the oil and beat until thick. Add the onion juice and poppy seeds and blend well. Store in the refrigerator.

Sour Cream Dressing
2 cups

1 cup sour cream	1 tablespoon sugar
1 tablespoon lemon juice	½ teaspoon prepared mustard
1 tablespoon cider vinegar	½ teaspoon salt

■ Whip the sour cream until fluffy. Add the remaining ingredients and chill.

Tasty Mayonnaise
2 cups

2 egg yolks	¾ teaspoon dry mustard
2 cups oil	¾ teaspoon paprika
2 tablespoons lemon juice	3 drops hot sauce
½ teaspoon salt	

■ In a deep, narrow bowl beat the egg yolks at high speed until thick and lemon colored. Add the oil, one tablespoon at a time, and beat until the mixture begins to thicken. Gradually add the lemon juice, beating until thickened. Add the remaining ingredients, stirring well. Spoon the mayonnaise into a glass or plastic container; cover and refrigerate. Do not store the mayonnaise in a metal container.

Thousand Island Dressing
1 cup

½ cup mayonnaise	1½ teaspoons chopped fresh parsley
¼ cup chili sauce	
1½ tablespoons coarsely chopped pimento-stuffed olives	1½ teaspoons chopped pimento
⅛ teaspoon onion powder	¼ teaspoon lemon juice

■ Combine all of the ingredients, stirring well. Chill before serving. Store in the refrigerator.

Main Dishes
■ ■ ■ ■ ■ ■ ■ ■ ■ ■ ■

LEMON-HERB ROAST CHICKEN
8 servings

Salt and pepper
2 teaspoons oregano
1 teaspoon tarragon
2 3-pound chickens

1 clove garlic, split
2 lemons, quartered
2 small onions

■ Sprinkle salt, pepper, and herbs inside each chicken cavity, and over the outside. Rub with garlic, lemon, and onion, and then place inside the cavities. Place the chickens in a shallow roasting pan. Bake at 350° for 1 hour to 1 hour and 15 minutes, or until tender.

BARBECUED CHICKEN
6 to 8 servings

2 medium chickens, cut up
½ teaspoon salt
1 tablespoon pepper
¼ cup lemon juice
½ cup butter
½ cup soy sauce

½ cup Worcestershire sauce
1½ tablespoons celery flakes
1½ tablespoons parsley flakes
2 tablespoons chili sauce
Lemon slices for garnish

■ Arrange the chicken in a shallow dish. Combine the remaining ingredients except the lemon slices and completely cover the chicken. Marinate overnight. About 3 hours before dinner preheat the oven to 350° and bake the chicken and sauce mixture uncovered for about 2½ hours. During baking, arrange the lemon slices over the chicken.

BUTTERMILK-PECAN CHICKEN
8 servings

¾ cup butter, melted
1 cup buttermilk
1 egg, slightly beaten
1 cup all-purpose flour
1 cup ground pecans

1 tablespoon paprika
1 tablespoon salt
⅛ teaspoon pepper
3½ pounds chicken, cut up
½ cup pecan halves

■ In a large shallow baking dish melt the butter in the oven. Remove and set aside.

In a shallow dish combine the buttermilk and egg. In a separate bowl combine the flour, ground pecans, sesame seeds, paprika, salt, and pepper. Coat the chicken in the buttermilk mixture and then in the flour mixture. Arrange the chicken skin side up in the baking dish, turning each piece to coat both sides with butter. Sprinkle with the pecan halves. Bake at 350° for about 1½ hours, until the chicken is browned.

CALICO CHICKEN

4 servings

2 chicken breasts, boned and cubed
2 tablespoons shortening
1 10¾-ounce can creamy chicken mushroom soup
⅓ cup milk

¼ teaspoon Italian Seasoning
1 8-ounce can mixed vegetables
1 tablespoon chopped parsley

■ In a skillet brown the chicken in the shortening. Drain off the fat. Stir in the soup, milk, and seasoning. Cover and simmer for 30 minutes or until done, stirring occasionally. Add the vegetables and parsley, and heat thoroughly. Serve over cooked noodles or rice.

OLD-FASHIONED CHICKEN AND DUMPLINGS

4 to 6 servings

1 3-pound frying chicken
2 quarts water
2 teaspoons salt
½ teaspoon pepper
2 cups all-purpose flour

½ teaspoon baking soda
½ teaspoon salt
3 tablespoons shortening
¾ cup buttermilk

■ Place the chicken in a Dutch oven. Add the water and 2 teaspoons of salt. Bring to a boil. Cover, reduce the heat, and simmer for 1 hour or until tender. Remove the chicken from the broth and cool. Bone the chicken and cut the meat into bite-sized pieces. Bring the broth to a boil and add pepper.

Combine the flour, baking soda, and salt. Cut in the shortening. Add the buttermilk, stirring with a fork until moistened. Knead the dough 4 to 5 times, and pat to ½-inch thickness. Pinch off dough into 1½-inch pieces and drop into the boiling broth. Reduce the heat to medium-low, and cook for about 8 to 10 minutes, stirring occasionally. Stir in the chicken and serve.

CREAMED CHICKEN LIVERS
2 servings

4 slices bacon
2 tablespoons all-purpose
  flour
  Pepper to taste
½ pound chicken livers

1 tablespoon chopped onion
1 10½-ounce can cream of
  mushroom soup
¼ cup water
1 cup hot cooked rice

■ In a skillet fry the bacon until crisp. Reserve 2 table-spoons of drippings. Combine the flour and pepper and coat the livers. Brown the livers and onion in the bacon drippings. Cover and cook over low heat for 8 to 10 minutes. Stir together the soup and water, and pour over the liver mixture. Heat through, and serve over the rice. Top with bacon strips.

SMOTHERED CHICKEN

2 tablespoons vinegar
1 3½-pound broiler
4 ribs celery
4 potatoes, peeled and
  quartered

1 small onion, sliced
  Salt and pepper to taste

■ Place the vinegar in the bottom of a deep ovenproof cas-serole dish or Dutch oven with a cover. Add the chicken and surround with the vegetables. Add seasonings to taste. Cover tightly and roast at 350° for 1 hour. The meat will be moist and juicy without having a strong vinegar taste.

SOUTHERN FRIED CHICKEN

⅓ cup oil
1 3-pound chicken, cut up

Salt and pepper
1 cup all-purpose flour

■ In a large skillet heat the oil over medium heat. Rub the chicken pieces with salt and pepper, and coat with flour. Brown the chicken on all sides for about 15 minutes, then reduce the heat and cover the skillet. Cook for about 30 minutes or until done, turning once about halfway through cooking.

HOT BROWN
6 servings

¼ cup butter
4 tablespoons all-purpose flour
2 cups milk
¾ cup shredded Cheddar cheese
¼ teaspoon salt
½ teaspoon Worcestershire sauce

1 pound thinly sliced turkey
6 slices toast
3 tomatoes, sliced
10 strips bacon, partially cooked

■ In a small saucepan melt the butter and stir in the flour. Whisk in the milk and stir until thickened. Add the cheese, salt, and Worcestershire sauce, stirring until smooth. Arrange the turkey on the toast in a 9x3-inch baking dish. Top with the cheese sauce, tomato slices, and bacon. Bake at 425° for 20 minutes or until bubbly.

CORNED BEEF-CABBAGE CASSEROLE
4 servings

1 15-ounce can corned beef, diced
1 10¾-ounce can cream of celery soup

½ cup chopped onion
1 teaspoon dry mustard
4 cups coarsely chopped cabbage

■ Combine all of the ingredients and pour into a greased 1½-quart casserole dish. Cover and bake at 375° for 35 to 40 minutes.

OVEN HASH
4 servings

1½ cups coarsely ground
   cooked beef
1 cup coarsely ground
   cooked potatoes
½ cup coarsely chopped
   onion
¼ cup chopped parsley
1 teaspoon salt

Pepper to taste
2 teaspoons Worcestershire
   sauce
1 6-ounce can evaporated
   milk
⅓ cup slightly crushed corn
   flakes
1 tablespoon butter, melted

■ Combine the beef, potatoes, onion, parsley, salt, pepper, Worcestershire sauce, and evaporated milk. Turn into a greased 1-quart casserole dish. Combine the cornflakes and butter, and sprinkle over the hash. Bake at 350° for 30 minutes or until heated through. Serve with catsup and mustard.

BARBECUED BEEF
6 to 8 servings

1 4- to 5-pound beef roast,
   cooked
1 cup meat stock
1 cup catsup or chili sauce
1 tablespoon Worcestersire
   sauce
1 teaspoon salt

2 tablespoons brown sugar
1 tablespoon lemon juice
2 tablespoons vinegar
1 teaspoon celery salt
1 teaspoon onion salt

■ Shred the beef and place in a skillet. Add the meat stock, catsup, Worcestershire sauce, salt, brown sugar, lemon juice, vinegar, celery salt, and onion salt. Cook over low heat for about 30 minutes.

BEEF STROGANOFF
6 servings

1½ pounds thin sirloin steak
½ teaspoon salt
⅛ teaspoon garlic salt
½ teaspoon paprika
⅛ teaspoon pepper
1 small onion, chopped
¼ cup butter, melted

⅓ cup sliced mushrooms
1 cup beef bouillon
2 small bay leaves
2 teaspoons Worcestershire
   sauce
6 servings cooked rice
1 cup sour cream

■ Cut the steak into 2-inch cubes. Season with the salts, paprika, and pepper and brown with the onion in the butter, add the mushrooms and brown a few minutes longer. Add the bouillon, bay leaves, and Worcestershire sauce and simmer for 25 to 30 minutes. Place the rice on serving plates and top with the beef cubes. Add the sour cream to the sauce in the pan and heat, stirring constantly. Pour over the rice and meat.

CORN BREAD PIE
4 servings

¾ cup milk
¾ cup corn bread mix
1 tablespoon sugar
1 pound ground beef
1 large onion, chopped
1 10½-ounce can tomato
   soup

2 cups water
1 tablespoon chili powder
½ cup chopped green pepper
1 teaspoon salt
¾ teaspoon pepper

■ In a small bowl mix together the milk, corn bread mix, and sugar. Set aside. In a large skillet brown the beef and onion. Add the soup, water, and seasonings. Mix and simmer for 15 minutes. Pour into a 9-inch baking dish or ovenproof skillet and top with the cornbread batter. Bake at 350° for 18 to 20 minutes.

Horseradish Meat Loaf
6 to 8 servings

1½ pounds ground beef	1 teaspooon mustard
½ pound ground pork	1 teaspoon salt
¼ cup grated onion	⅛ teaspoon pepper
2 eggs	¼ to ⅓ cup catsup
1 cup dry bread crumbs	⅓ cup milk
⅓ cup horseradish	

■ Combine all of the ingredients thoroughly and shape into a loaf. Score the top diagonally. Bake at 350° for 1 hour or until done.

Savory Steak
4 servings

2½ pounds round steak	1½ cups hot water
Flour	½ teaspoon prepared
Bacon drippings	mustard
¾ teaspoon salt	2 tablespoons catsup
Pepper to taste	1 small onion

■ Pound as much flour into the steak as possible. In a skillet heat the bacon drippings and brown the steak. Season with salt and pepper. Combine the hot water, mustard, and catsup, and pour over the meat. Add the onion, cover tightly, and simmer about 1½ hours or until tender. Place the steaks on serving plates and top with the sauce.

Braised Beef with Vegetables
4 servings

2 pounds beef round or	1 cup diced onion
shoulder	1 cup diced celery
Salt and pepper	2½ cups boiling water
Flour	½ cup catsup
1 cup diced carrot	Potatoes, peeled
1 cup diced turnip	

■ Sprinkle the beef with salt and pepper. Dredge with flour and brown in butter. Place the beef in a casserole dish or deep baking pan and add the carrot, turnip, onion, and celery. Combine the boiling water and catsup, and pour ⅔ of the mixture over the meat and vegetables. Cover and bake at 325° for about 2 hours, basting every 30 minutes with the remaining liquid. Turn the meat over once during cooking. During the last hour of cooking place the potatoes around the meat and cook until tender.

Veal pot roast
6 servings

4 tablespoons butter
1 6-pound veal rump roast
2 medium onions, chopped
2 cups sour cream
3 cups chicken stock

2 teaspoons dill weed
1 teaspoon seasoned salt
¼ teaspoon red pepper flakes

■ In a Dutch oven melt the butter and brown the roast. Remove the roast and sauté the onion in the remaining butter until light brown. Stir in the sour cream, 2 cups of chicken stock, and the seasonings. Add the roast to the pot and baste with the sauce. Cover and simmer for 2 to 3 hours or until the meat is fork tender. Add more chicken stock as needed. Serve the sauce separately.

Southern Steak Barbecue

6 servings

¼ cup (½ stick) butter,
  softened
2 tablespoons dry mustard
2 teaspoons salt
2 teaspoons sugar
¾ teaspoon paprika
¼ teaspoon pepper
2 pounds sirloin steak,
  1-inch thick

¼ cup olive oil
2 tablespoons Worcestershire
  sauce
2 tablespoons catsup
¾ teaspoon sugar
¾ teaspoon salt

■ Combine the butter, dry mustard, salt, sugar, paprika, and pepper. Spread half on one side of the meat. In a large skillet, brown the meat buttered side down. As the meat browns, spread the remaining butter over the top. Turn and brown. Remove and place the steak in a broiler pan. Combine the remaining ingredients and the skillet drippings, and brush on the steak. Broil 5 inches from the heat for 5 to 7 minutes on each side, brushing frequently with the sauce.

Roasted Beef Ribs

4 to 6 servings

6 beef ribs (5 to 6 pounds)
1 cup oil
½ cup Worcestershire sauce
Juice of 2 lemons

1 teaspoon garlic salt
1 teaspoon salt
1 teaspoon black pepper
2 medium onions, sliced

■ Trim the fat from the ribs. Place in a 9x13-inch baking dish. Combine the remaining ingredients and pour over the ribs. Cover and refrigerate overnight.

Drain and discard the marinade. Bake the ribs at 350° for 30 minutes or until tender. Remove from the oven and place on a hot grill. Grill the ribs for 10 minutes on each side, until crisp and brown. Serve hot.

LIVER AND GRAVY
4 servings

¼ cup all-purpose flour
¼ teaspoon salt
⅛ teaspoon pepper
1 pound thinly sliced beef
  liver
2 tablespoons bacon
  drippings
2 medium onions, chopped

3 tablespoons bacon
  drippings
1 tablespoon all-purpose
  flour
1½ cups water
1 teaspoon salt
¼ teaspoon pepper

■ Combine ¼ cup of flour, ¼ teaspoon of salt, and ⅛ teaspoon of pepper. Coat the liver in the flour mixture and brown in 2 tablespoons of bacon drippings. Remove the liver to a shallow 1½-quart baking dish.

In a skillet sauté the onion in 3 tablespoons of bacon drippings. Add 1 tablespoon of flour, stirring occasionally until brown. Gradually add the water, stirring until smooth. Stir in the seasonings and pour over the liver. Bake at 350° for 40 minutes or until the gravy has thickened and the liver is tender.

Tennessee Pot Roast

8 to 10 servings

3 tablespoons all-purpose
  flour
1 teaspoon salt
1/4 teaspoon pepper
1/4 teaspoon allspice
1 3- to 3 1/2-pound boneless
  beef roast
2 tablespoons shortening

2 cups apple juice
1 beef bouillon cube, crushed
4 carrots, cut in 3-inch pieces
1 cup celery, cut in 2-inch
  pieces
3 medium potatoes, quartered
1 teaspoon thyme

■ Combine the flour, salt, pepper, and allspice. Dredge the meat, reserving excess flour. Brown the meat in shortening, and remove to a Dutch oven or large pan. Heat the apple juice and crushed bouillon cube and stir to dissolve. Pour the liquid over the meat, cover tightly and cook slowly for 2 hours. Add the vegetables and thyme, cover, and continue cooking for 30 minutes or until the vegetables are tender. Remove the meat and vegetables to a warm platter.

Roast leg of lamb

1 3- to 5-pound leg of lamb
3 to 4 cloves garlic
1 teaspoon whole cloves

Juice of 1 lemon
Salt and pepper

■ Remove the excess fat and the thin protective covering from the leg of lamb. Score the meat and fill the openings with the garlic cloves. Rub the meat with the lemon juice, sprinkle with salt and pepper, and stick the cloves into the meat. Wrap in foil and place in an oven roaster. Bake at 350° for 30 to 40 minutes per pound.

SAUSAGE
20 servings

 4 pounds freshly ground pork   ¾ tablespoon cayenne pepper
¾ tablespoon salt   ⅛ cup finely chopped garlic
½ tablespoon pepper
¾ tablespoon sage

■ Combine all of the ingredients by hand and form into patties. Cook in a skillet until browned.

CABBAGE WITH SAUSAGE
6 servings

2½ pounds green cabbage   2 eggs
  1 pound sausage, crumbled   2 cups milk
  1 large onion, chopped   Cracker crumbs

■ Shred the cabbage and cook in salted water for 15 minutes. Cook the sausage and remove from the skillet. In the sausage drippings, cook the onion until clear. Set the onion aside and reserve the drippings. Beat the eggs and add to the milk. Layer the cabbage, sausage and onions in the casserole. Repeat the layers, and pour the egg mixture over all. Sprinkle crumbs over all and drizzle with 2 or 3 tablespoons of sausage drippings. Cover and cook at 350° for 45 minutes.

PORK CHOPS WITH APPLES
4 servings

2 tablespoons oil	1 teaspoon salt
2 cooking apples, cored and	⅛ teaspoon pepper
thickly sliced	1½ cups apple juice
4 ½-inch thick pork chops	1 tablespoon cornstarch
2 green onions, sliced	¼ cup light cream or milk

■ In a large skillet heat the oil and cook the apples until tender; about 5 minutes. Remove and keep warm. Brown the pork chops in the skillet for about 10 minutes. Add green onions, salt, pepper, and 1¼ cups of apple juice; bring to a boil. Reduce heat, cover, simmer 15 to 20 minutes or until the meat is tender. Remove the chops and keep warm. In a small cup, blend the cornstarch and remaining apple juice until smooth; gradually stir into the liquid in the skillet. Add the cream, stirring until the gravy is slightly thickened. Return the chops and apple slices to the skillet and heat.

HONEY GLAZED PORK ROAST WITH SWEET POTATOES
8 servings

6 pound pork loin roast	½ cup honey
Salt and pepper to taste	3 teaspoons grated orange
6 sweet potatoes	rind

■ Rub the roast well with salt and pepper. Cut slits in the fat with a sharp knife. Roast fat side up in a shallow pan at 350° for 2 hours. Quarter and cook the potatoes in water until almost tender; place around the roast and drizzle with honey and orange peel. Increase the heat to 400° and cook 20 minutes longer, until the meat and potatoes are golden brown.

Pork barbecue

1 teaspoon salt	1 green pepper, chopped
1 teaspoon black pepper	2 large pods red hot pepper
1 teaspoon paprika	(or 2 tablespoons crushed)
4 tablespoons sugar	2 cups vinegar
2 tablespoons Worcestershire	2 cups water
sauce	1 cup tomato catsup
1 onion, chopped	1/2 cup butter
3 stalks celery, chopped	Shredded cooked pork roast

■ In a large saucepan combine all of the ingredients except the meat and cook for about 10 minutes. Strain and pour over the meat, and cook for about 30 minutes.

Ham loaf with horseradish sauce
6 to 8 servings

3/4 pound lean pork, ground	2 teaspoons vinegar
1 pound smoked ham,	1 1/2 teaspoons prepared
ground	mustard
1/2 cup milk	1 teaspoon salt
1/2 cup dry bread crumbs	1/8 teaspoon Worcestershire
1 egg, slightly beaten	sauce
6 tablespoons brown sugar	Dash cayenne pepper
2 tablespoons water	Dash paprika
2 tablespoons vinegar	1/4 cup heavy cream,
1 teaspoon dry mustard	whipped
2 tablespoons horseradish	

■ Combine the pork, ham, milk, bread crumbs, and egg. Shape into a loaf and place in a shallow baking dish. Bake at 350° for 45 to 60 minutes. Combine the brown sugar, water, 2 tablespoons of vinegar, and the dry mustard. Baste the loaf occasionally. Combine the remaining ingredients and serve with the Ham Loaf.

Pan-Fried Catfish
4 servings

2 to 3 pounds catfish
1 cup shortening or oil
2 tablespoons salt

½ cup cornmeal
½ cup buttermilk

■ Cut the fish into serving pieces. Heat the shortening in a skillet over medium heat. Combine the salt and cornmeal. Dip the fish in the buttermilk and then roll in the cornmeal mixture. Fry in hot shortening for 3 minutes or until golden brown.

Fried Shrimp
4 to 6 servings

2 pounds medium shrimp, peeled and deveined
Juice of lemon
Flour for dredging
Salt to taste

Pepper to taste
2 eggs, beaten
1 cup cornmeal
Oil for deep frying

■ Squeeze the lemon juice over the shrimp and let stand for a few minutes. Combine the flour, salt and pepper, and dredge the shrimp. Set aside for about 30 minutes. Dip the shrimp in the beaten egg and then the cornmeal.

In a large skillet, fry the shrimp in oil until golden brown, about 3 to 5 minutes. Drain on paper towels.

Shrimp and Corn Pie
6 servings

2 cups corn
2 eggs, slightly beaten
1 tablespoon butter
½ cup milk
1 cup cooked shrimp

1 teaspoon Worcestershire sauce
Salt and pepper to taste
Mace to taste

■ To the grated corn add the eggs, butter, milk, shrimp and seasonings. Bake in a buttered casserole at 300° for 30 minutes.

Vegetables
■■■■■■■■■■

Quick hot cinnamon applesauce
4 servings

1 24-ounce jar (2¾ cups)
   applesauce
½ cup packed brown sugar

½ cup sugar
2 teaspoons cinnamon
   Dash nutmeg
2 tablespoons butter

■ In a saucepan combine and mix all of the ingredients and cook over medium heat 4 to 5 minutes.

BAKED BEANS
6 servings

2 green peppers, finely
  chopped
1 small onion, finely chopped
½ cup brown sugar
½ cup catsup

1 teaspoon mustard
1 teaspoon Worcestershire
  sauce
1 16-ounce can pork and
  beans
6 slices bacon

■ In a casserole dish combine all of the ingredients except
the bacon slices. Arrange the bacon over the mixture and
bake uncovered at 325° for 1½ to 2 hours.

HOPPING JOHN
8 servings

2 cups black-eyed peas
  Water
1 tablespoon bacon drippings
1 cup coarsely chopped onion
1 cup long grain rice

1 teaspoon salt
¼ teaspoon pepper
¼ pound thickly sliced bacon,
  cooked

■ Wash and sort the peas. In a medium saucepan, combine
the peas and 4 cups of water and bring to boiling. Reduce
the heat and simmer, covered, for 45 minutes. Drain the
peas, reserving the liquid. Set both the peas and the liquid
aside.

In a Dutch oven sauté the onion in the bacon drippings
until golden. Add water to the reserved liquid from the
peas to make 4 cups. Add the water, peas, rice, salt, and
pepper to the onions and bring to a boil. Reduce the heat,
cover, simmer for about 35 to 40 minutes, until the peas
and rice are tender and the liquid is absorbed. Crumble the
bacon and stir into the Hopping John.

Broccoli with horseradish dressing

½ cup water
¼ teaspoon salt
1 10-ounce package frozen
   broccoli

½ cup salad dressing
1 teaspoon sugar
2 tablespoons horseradish
   mustard

■ Bring the water and salt to a boil. Add the frozen broccoli and return to a boil. Reduce to a simmer and cook for 5 to 8 minutes. Combine the remaining ingredients and serve over the broccoli.

Marinated carrots

2 pounds carrots, peeled and
   sliced
2 medium onions, diced
2 green peppers, chopped
1 10½-ounce can tomato
   soup
¾ cup vinegar

½ cup oil
1 teaspoon Worcestershire
   sauce
1 teaspoon prepared mustard
¾ cup sugar

■ Cook the carrots in salted water until tender. Drain. In a casserole or serving dish arrange the carrots, onions, and peppers in layers. Combine the remaining ingredients and pour over the carrots. Refrigerate for 24 hours before serving.

CAULIFLOWER WITH CHEESE SAUCE
8 servings

1 large head cauliflower
  Salt
4 tablespoons melted butter
4 tablespoons flour

2½ cups milk
½ teaspoon pepper
1 cup grated cheese
12 slices bacon, cooked and
  crumbled

■ Soak the cauliflower in cold salted water for 20 minutes. In a large saucepan add the cauliflower to boiling salted water and cook, uncovered, for 10 to 20 minutes or until the cauliflower is tender. Drain.

In a double boiler or heavy saucepan over low heat combine the melted butter and flour, stirring until combined. Add the milk, 1 teaspoon of salt and the pepper. Stir frequently until thickened, and add the cheese. Stir until the cheese melts, and pour over the cooked cauliflower. Top with crumbled bacon.

CORN AND TOMATO CASSEROLE
8 servings

6 ears fresh corn
1 medium onion, chopped
1 medium green pepper,
  chopped
4 tablespoons butter, melted

5 medium tomatoes,
  sliced ½-inch thick
1 teaspoon salt
½ teaspoon pepper
1 cup soft breadcrumbs

■ Cut the corn from the cobs. In a large skillet sauté the onion, green pepper, and corn in 2 tablespoons of butter for 5 minutes. Place half of the corn mixture in a 2-quart casserole and top with half of the tomato slices.Season with half of the salt and pepper. Top with the remaining corn mixture and tomatoes. Combine the breadcrumbs and melted butter and sprinkle over the tomato slices. Bake at 375° for 30 minutes.

CORN PUDDING
8 to 10 servings

10 ears corn
  3 tablespoons real butter
  2 tablespoons all-purpose
    flour
  1 pint whole milk

3 egg yolks, beaten
3 tablespoons sugar
1 teaspoon salt
3 egg whites, beaten

■ Shave off the tips of the corn kernels and scrape the pulp from the cobs. Melt the butter and add the flour, stirring until smooth. Add the milk, beaten yolks, sugar, and salt. Fold in the egg whites. Bake in a greased casserole at 350° until firm, about 45 minutes.

DEVILED EGGS
12 to 15 servings

12 hard-cooked eggs
  1 tablespoon vinegar
  1 4½-ounce can deviled ham
⅓ cup mayonnaise
  2 teaspoons prepared
    mustard

1 tablespoon sweet pickle
relish
Salt and pepper to taste
Paprika

■ Slice the eggs in half lengthwise, and remove the yolks. Mash the yolks and sprinkle with vinegar. Add the remaining ingredients except the paprika and stir well. Stuff the egg whites with the yolk mixture and garnish with paprika.

CREAM-STYLE GREEN BEANS
4 servings

*1 10-ounce package frozen
green beans*
*1 3-ounce package cream
cheese, softened*

1 tablespoon milk
¼ teaspoon celery seed
¼ teaspoon salt

■ Prepare the green beans according to package directions and drain. Combine the remaining ingredients and blend thoroughly. Add to the beans and heat through.

BAKED LIMAS WITH SOUR CREAM
6 servings

1 pound dried limas
3 teaspoons salt
½ cup butter
¾ cup brown sugar

1 tablespoon dry mustard
1 tablespoon molasses
1 cup sour cream

■ Soak the lima beans overnight in water. Drain and cover with fresh water. Add 1 teaspoon salt and cook until tender, 30 to 45 minutes. Drain again and rinse under hot water. Place in a casserole and dot with butter. Combine the brown sugar, dry mustard and remaining salt, and sprinkle over the beans. Stir in the molasses and pour the sour cream over all. Mix tenderly. Bake at 350° for 1 hour.

Baked Macaroni and Cheese

6 servings

1 7-ounce package (2 cups
    uncooked) elbow macaroni
2 tablespoons margarine
2 tablespoons all-purpose
    flour
1 teaspoon dry mustard
    (optional)

1 teaspoon salt
2½ cups milk
2 cups shredded sharp
    Cheddar cheese

■ Prepare the macaroni according to package directions and drain.

In a medium saucepan, melt the margarine and stir in the flour, mustard, and salt. Gradually stir in the milk. Cook and stir until the mixture thickens slightly. Remove from heat. Add 1½ cups of cheese and stir until melted. Stir in the cooked macaroni. Turn into a greased 1½-quart shallow baking dish. Top with the remaining cheese. Bake at 375° for 20 to 25 minutes or until bubbly.

Fried Okra

4 servings

 4 cups sliced okra
½ cup milk
¼ teaspoon salt

¼ teaspoon pepper
¾ cup cornmeal
    Oil

■ In a shallow dish combine the okra, milk, and seasonings. Let the okra stand for 1 hour or until most of the milk is absorbed. Dredge in cornmeal and fry the okra pieces in deep hot oil until browned. Drain on paper towels and serve hot.

Stewed Okra and Tomatoes
4 to 6 servings

1 16-ounce can tomatoes with juice	2 tablespoons butter or bacon drippings
1 teaspoon salt	1/2 pound okra
1/2 teaspoon white pepper	2 teaspoons cornstarch
	2 teaspoons water

■ In a heavy saucepan combine the first 4 ingredients. Simmer covered for 10 minutes. Wash, trim, and slice the okra into 1/4-inch pieces. Add the okra to the tomatoes, and simmer for 5 minutes. If the stew is too runny, mix together the cornstarch and water, and add to the stew. Season to taste.

Green Onions

6 large green onions	1 cup water
1/4 cup bacon drippings	1 teaspoon salt

■ Chop the onions up coarsely, head and blades. In a skillet melt the bacon drippings and add the onions and salted water. Cook until the onions are tender and the water is absorbed.

Hash Brown Potatoes

2 tablespoons fat	1 teaspoon salt
1 1/2 tablespoons all-purpose flour	4 medium cooked potatoes, finely chopped
Pepper to taste	2 tablespoons milk

■ In a frying pan, heat the fat. Stir the flour, pepper, and salt into the potato and press it down firmly into the pan.

Add the milk. Brown the potato slowly, allowing 30 minutes for cooking. Turn it out as an omelet is turned, and serve hot.

Poke casserole
4 servings

½ cup margarine, melted
6 eggs, lightly beaten
1 tablespoon all-purpose flour
1 pint cottage cheese
1 8-ounce package Cracker Barrel Sharp Cheddar cheese, cubed

1 4-ounce package grated Cheddar cheese
2 cups parboiled poke, drained and squeezed

■ Combine all of the ingredients, adding the poke last. Bake in a greased casserole dish at 350° for 1 hour. Let the casserole stand for 20 minutes before serving.

Hash brown potato casserole
8 to 10 servings

2 cups shredded American or Cheddar cheese
1 10¾-ounce can cream of chicken soup
1 cup sour cream
1 cup finely chopped onion (optional)
¼ cup butter, melted

¼ teaspoon salt
¼ teaspoon pepper
1 32-ounce package frozen loose-pack hash brown potatoes, thawed
1 cup corn flakes, crushed
1 tablespoon butter, melted

■ In a large mixing bowl combine the shredded cheese, chicken soup, sour cream, chopped onion, ¼ cup of butter, salt and pepper. Mix well. Fold in the thawed hash brown potatoes. Turn mixture into a greased 9 x 13 baking dish. Toss together the cornflakes and 1 tablespoon of melted butter and sprinkle over the potato mixture. Bake at 350° for about 1 hour or until the casserole is golden brown and the potatoes are tender.

Roast potatoes
12 servings

12 medium potatoes
1 quart oil (approximately)
Salt

■ Place the potatoes in a large pan, cover with water and boil for 20 minutes.

Place enough oil in a roasting pan to come halfway up on the potatoes. Place the pan in a preheated 450° oven and allow it to get very hot. Place the potatoes in the hot oil very carefully with a spoon. Roast the potatoes for 45 minutes, turning every 15 minutes until brown. Salt the potatoes when they are removed from the oil. The potatoes can be kept in a warm oven for awhile after being removed from the oil.

Scalloped potatoes

2 ½-inch thick slices smoked ham
1 10¾-ounce can cream of mushroom soup
1 cup sour cream
1 teaspoon salt

½ teaspoon white pepper
8 medium potatoes, thickly sliced
1 cup sliced onions
1 cup shredded Cheddar cheese

■ Cut the ham into 8 serving pieces. Combine the soup, sour cream, salt and pepper. In a buttered 3-quart casserole, alternate layers of ham, potatoes, and onions with the sour cream mixture, ending with sour cream. Top with shredded cheese. Cover the casserole loosely with aluminum foil and bake at 325° for 2½ hours.

SWEET POTATO PONE
10 to 12 servings

4 cups peeled and shredded
   sweet potatoes
Rind of 1 orange, grated
1½ cups sugar
½ teaspoon salt
¾ cup butter, softened

1 cup milk
2 eggs, lightly beaten
1 teaspoon cinnamon
¼ teaspoon nutmeg
1 teaspoon vanilla extract
   (optional)

■ In a large mixing bowl, combine the sweet potatoes and orange rind. Add the remaining ingredients and blend thoroughly. Spoon the mixture into a greased 8-inch square baking dish. Bake at 325° for 1½ hours. Serve hot or cold.

SINFULLY RICH SWEET POTATOES
6 servings

3 cups mashed sweet
   potatoes
¾ cup sugar
2 eggs, beaten
1 cup evaporated milk
¼ cup margarine

1 teaspoon vanilla extract
1 cup brown sugar
⅓ cup margarine, melted
1 cup flaked coconut
1 cup pecans, chopped

■ In a large bowl, beat the sweet potatoes, sugar, eggs, evaporated milk, ¼ cup of margarine, and vanilla. Pour the mixture into a greased 2-quart casserole. Combine the brown sugar, ⅓ cup of margarine, coconut and pecans and mix until crumbly. Sprinkle over the potato mixture. Bake at 375° for 30 minutes.

Squash puffs

1 cup mashed cooked squash	1 teaspoon baking powder
1 egg, beaten	1/2 teaspoon salt
1/2 cup all-purpose flour	1 medium onion, finely
1/2 cup cornmeal	chopped
	Oil

■ In a small bowl combine the mashed squash and egg, stirring well. In a separate bowl combine the flour, cornmeal, baking powder and salt. Add the squash mixture and onion, stirring until blended. Drop the squash mixture by level tablespoons into hot oil. Cook until golden brown. Drain on paper towels.

Acorn squash with peas
4 servings

2 medium acorn squash	2 10-ounce packages frozen
4 tablespoons butter	peas
	Red pepper slices

■ Cut the squash in half and place cut-side down on a baking sheet. Bake at 350° for 30 minutes. Turn cut-side up and place a tablespoon of butter in each cavity. Bake for 15 minutes or until fork tender. Prepare the peas according to the package directions. Fill each squash half with peas and garnish with red pepper slices.

Fried tomatoes
4 servings

4 medium tomatoes (half	2 1/2 teaspoons sugar
ripe)	1/4 teaspoon pepper
1/2 cup all-purpose flour	3/4 cup evaporated milk
2 1/2 teaspoons salt	Oil

■ Wash the tomatoes and cut unpeeled into 3/4-inch thick slices. Drain on paper towels. Combine the flour, salt, sugar, and pepper and dust the tomatoes in the flour mixture. Add milk to the remaining mixture to make a thick batter. Dip the floured tomatoes in the batter and fry in hot oil, ½ inch deep, until golden brown, turning once.

FIERY MARINATED TOMATOES
10 servings

6 medium tomatoes, peeled
  and quartered
1 medium onion, sliced
1 medium green pepper, cut
  into strips
1 large cucumber, peeled and
  sliced
¾ cup cider vinegar

¼ cup water
1 tablespoon plus 2
  teaspoons sugar
1½ teaspoons celery salt
1½ teaspoons mustard seeds
½ teaspoon salt
½ teaspoon red pepper
⅛ teaspoon pepper

■ In a large bowl combine the vegetables. In a small saucepan combine the vinegar, water, and seasonings. Bring to a boil and boil for 1 minute. Pour over the vegetables, cover, and chill overnight.

HOMESTYLE STEWED TOMATOES
8 servings

1 medium green pepper,
  chopped
1 large onion, chopped
1 medium celery stalk,
  chopped
2 tablespoons oil
12 medium tomatoes, peeled

1 tablespoon light brown
  sugar
¾ teaspoon salt
½ teaspoon dried thyme
  leaves
¼ teaspoon pepper

■ Reserve 1 tablespoon of green pepper for garnish. In a large saucepan sauté the onion, green pepper, and celery in oil until tender. Cut each tomato into 8 wedges and reserve ⅓ of the wedges. Add the wedges to the sautéed vegetables with the seasonings and bring to a boil. Reduce the heat and cook uncovered for 45 minutes, stirring occasionally. Add the reserved tomato wedges and cook about 20 minutes or until the mixture is slightly thickened. Serve in bowls garnished with chopped green pepper.

Tomato Pudding

1 quart canned tomatoes
1 ½ cups brown sugar

¼ cup butter (or 1 tablespoon
  bacon drippings)
6 slices bread

■ In a saucepan bring the tomatoes, sugar, and butter to a boil. Break the bread into pieces and add to the tomato mixture. Add extra bread until all of the liquid is absorbed.

Turnips
6 servings

3 pounds white turnips
¼ pound bacon, diced
⅔ cup finely chopped onion
1 tablespoon all-purpose
  flour

1 cup canned beef bouillon
1 teaspoon sugar
¼ teaspoon rubbed sage
¼ teaspoon black pepper

■ Peel and cube or slice the turnips. Drop into boiling water and cook for 5 minutes. Drain. Sauté the bacon and add the remaining ingredients. Cook until tender.

Fried Mush with Sausage

Salt and pepper
3 cups cornmeal
Water

1 ½ cups sausage, cooked and
  crumbled
2 eggs, beaten
2 cups bread crumbs

■ Combine the salt, pepper, and cornmeal. Add enough water to make a medium-textured batter. Add the sausage and pour into a plastic loaf pan. Refrigerate overnight. Unmold and slice the mush. Dip each slice into the beaten egg, then roll in the bread crumbs. Deep fry these until golden brown. Serve plain or with syrup.

DIRTY RICE
6 servings

1 pound pork sausage
1 medium-large onion,
  chopped
1 green pepper, chopped
1 clove garlic, chopped
½ pound fresh mushrooms,
  chopped

5 chicken livers, chopped
4 green onions, chopped
½ cup chopped parsley
  Salt to taste
2 cups cooked rice

■ In a skillet brown the sausage. Add the remaining ingredients except the rice. Cook over medium low heat until the vegetables are soft and lightly browned. Add the cooked rice and stir well. Place in covered casserole and bake at 350° for 20 to 30 minutes.

Oven Steamed Rice
4 servings

1½ cups rice
1½ teaspoons salt
   Dash pepper

2 tablespoons butter
3½ cups boiling water
¼ cup sliced green onions

■ In a 2-quart saucepan combine the rice and seasonings, and dot with butter. Add the boiling water and stir. Cover and bake at 350° for 45 minutes. Add the onions.

Wild Rice
8 to 10 servings

¼ cup butter
1 cup wild rice
½ cup slivered almonds
1 tablespoon chopped chives
  or green onions

1 tablespoon chopped green
  pepper
½ pound sliced fresh
  mushrooms
3 cups chicken broth

■ In a heavy saucepan over medium heat, cook all of the ingredients except the chicken broth and stir until the rice turns yellow. Add the broth and turn into a baking dish. Bake at 350° for about 1 hour.

Breads

■ ■ ■ ■ ■ ■ ■

Southern homemade buttermilk BISCUITS
16 to 20 biscuits

2 cups all-purpose flour
2 teaspoons baking powder
½ teaspoon baking soda

½ teaspoon salt
¼ cup shortening
1 cup buttermilk

■ Sift together the flour, baking powder, baking soda, and salt. Cut in the shortening, add the buttermilk, and mix well. Turn out on a floured board. Roll out and cut. Bake at 450° until browned.

BEATEN BISCUITS
24 biscuits

3 cups sifted all-purpose flour   1/3 cup cold shortening
1 teaspoon salt   1/2 cup cold milk

■ Sift the flour with the salt, and cut in the shortening. Add the milk and mix to a very stiff dough. Place on a floured board and beat with a rolling pin for 30 minutes, folding in the edges after each stroke. Roll 1/3-inch thick and cut with a biscuit cutter. Place on a greased baking sheet and prick with a fork. Bake at 400° for 20 minutes.

CREAM BISCUITS
20 biscuits

4 cups all-purpose flour   1/2 cup salted butter
2 tablespoons baking powder   1 pint plus 1 tablespoon
1 teaspoon salt   heavy cream

■ In a large bowl stir together the flour, baking powder, and salt. Cut in the butter until the mixture resembles coarse meal. Gradually add the cream. Knead just long enough to make a stiff dough. Do not overwork. Roll out to 1/2-inch thickness. Cut into squares and place on a greased baking sheet. Bake at 400° for 18 minutes, or until puffed and browned. Serve warm.

EGG BREAD
10 to 12 servings

1 cup milk   1 teaspoon baking soda
1 cup water   2 cups buttermilk
2 cups cornmeal   2 tablespoons shortening
3 eggs   1/4 cup cornmeal
1 teaspoon salt

■ In a saucepan, combine the milk and water. Bring to a boil and add 2 cups of cornmeal, stirring constantly to make a mush. Beat the eggs until very light, and add the salt. Stir the soda into the buttermilk. Combine the cornmeal, eggs, and buttermilk mixtures. Melt the shortening in a large iron skillet. Pour the hot shortening into the batter. Mix, and stir in ¼ cup of cornmeal. Pour the batter into the hot skillet and bake at 375° for 25 to 30 minutes.

JAM-FILLED CORN MUFFINS

12 large muffins

3¾ cups all-purpose flour	2 eggs
1¼ cups yellow cornmeal	½ cup oil
5 teaspoons baking powder	⅛ teaspoon nutmeg
½ cup sugar	1½ cups buttermilk
1 teaspoon salt	⅓ cup strawberry jam

■ Combine the flour, cornmeal, baking powder, sugar, and salt. With an electric mixer add the eggs, oil, and nutmeg. Beat at medium speed while adding the buttermilk. Fill greased muffin tins, and press a teaspoonful of jam into each. Place the muffin pan on a baking sheet. Bake at 400° in the center of the oven for 30 minutes. Cool in the pan.

CORN LIGHT BREAD

2 tablespoons shortening	1 ¼-ounce package active dry
2 cups self-rising cornmeal	yeast
½ cup self-rising flour	2 cups buttermilk
¾ cup sugar	

■ Melt the shortening in a loaf pan. In a separate bowl combine the cornmeal, flour, sugar. Sift together and add the yeast. Add the buttermilk and mix well. Add the melted shortening to the batter and stir to combine. Pour the mixture into the loaf pan. Bake at 375° for 45 minutes.

CORN STICKS
6 corn sticks

¾ cup cornmeal	1 cup milk
1 cup all-purpose flour	1 egg, well beaten
3 teaspoons baking powder	¼ cup shortening, melted
¾ teaspoon salt	½ cup boiling hot hominy

■ Sift the dry ingredients into a mixing bowl. Add the milk, egg, shortening, and hominy. Mix well. Turn into a buttered cornstick pan. Bake at 350° for 20 minutes.

SOUTHERN SPOONBREAD

2 cups white cornmeal	2 egg yolks, lightly beaten
2½ cups boiling water	1 teaspoon baking soda
1½ tablespoons butter, melted	1½ cups buttermilk
1½ teaspoons salt	2 egg whites, beaten stiff

■ Add the cornmeal gradually to the boiling water and let stand a few minutes. Add the butter, salt and egg yolks. Dissolve the baking soda in the buttermilk and add to the cornmeal mixture. Fold in the egg whites. Turn into a buttered casserole. Bake at 375° for 40 minutes.

HUSH PUPPIES

1 cup cornmeal	½ cup cracker meal
½ cup all-purpose flour	1 pinch sugar
1 egg	1 teaspoon salt
1 heaping teaspoon baking powder	1 cup grated onion
	Milk as needed

■ Combine the ingredients and add enough milk to make a soft ball. Drop by spoonful into deep fat.

Oatmeal Raisin Muffins
12 muffins

1 egg	*3 teaspoons baking powder*
½ cup oil	*1 teaspoon salt*
¾ cup milk	*½ teaspoon nutmeg*
1 cup all-purpose flour	*½ teaspoon cinnamon*
1 cup oatmeal	*½ cup raisins*
½ cup brown sugar	

■ Beat the egg. Stir in the oil and milk. Combine the remaining ingredients and stir into the liquids until just moistened. Fill greased muffin cups ⅔ full. Bake at 400° for 20 minutes.

Oyster Dressing

1 cup butter	*1 teaspoon pepper*
2 onions, chopped	*½ teaspoon poultry seasoning*
3 cups chopped celery	*½ clove garlic*
1 cup chopped mushrooms	*¼ teaspoon thyme*
2 cups chopped oysters	*¼ teaspoon sage*
8 to 9 cups soft bread crumbs	*¼ teaspoon oregano*
1½ cups broth from giblets	*3 tablespoons chopped parsley*
1 teaspoon salt	

■ In a skillet melt the butter and sauté the onions and celery until golden. Add the mushrooms and oysters; cook for 1 minute and remove from heat. Combine the bread crumbs, stock, and all of the seasonings and mix well. Bake in a greased pan at 350° or fill the body and neck cavities of the turkey, but do not pack. Roast according to the weight of the bird.

CORN BREAD-SAUSAGE-PECAN DRESSING
8 to 10 servings

7½ slices toasted bread,
   coarsely crumbled
6 cups cornbread crumbs
6 chicken-flavored bouillon
   cubes
4 cups boiling water
1 small onion, finely
   chopped
2 green peppers, finely
   chopped

2 stalks celery, chopped
¼ cup butter, melted
½ pound bulk pork sausage
1 cup pecans, finely chopped
1 teaspoon poultry seasoning
½ teaspoon salt
¼ teaspoon pepper
4 eggs, beaten

■ In a large bowl combine the bread crumbs and corn bread crumbs. Dissolve the bouillon cubes in the boiling water; pour over the crumb mixture and stir well. In a skillet sauté the onion, pepper, and celery in butter until tender. Add to the crumb mixture and stir well. Brown and drain the sausage, and stir with the remaining ingredients into the crumb mixture. Spoon into a lightly greased 13x9x2-inch baking dish and bake at 350° for about 45 minutes.

APPLE BUTTER BREAD
1 loaf

2 cups all-purpose flour
1 teaspoon baking powder
1/4 teaspoon baking soda
1 teaspoon cinnamon
1 1/4 teaspoon nutmeg
1/2 cup chopped pecans

1/2 cup raisins, boiled and
    drained
1 cup oil
3 eggs
1 cup sugar
3/4 cup apple butter

■ Sift together the flour, baking powder, baking soda, and spices. Stir in the pecans and raisins. In a large bowl cream together the oil, eggs, and sugar. Blend in the apple butter. Add the flour mixture to the creamed mixture and blend well. Pour into a 9x5-inch loaf pan. Bake at 375° for about 1 hour and 30 minutes.

BACON-CHEDDAR BREAD
3 loaves

1/2 pound lean bacon,
    chopped
2 cups all-purpose flour
1/2 cup yellow cornmeal
1 teaspoon salt
1/2 teaspoon baking soda
1 1/2 teaspoons baking powder
1 cup finely grated sharp
    Cheddar cheese

3 tablespoons minced fresh
    dill
1/4 cup shortening, softened
2 tablespoons sugar
2 large eggs, beaten lightly
1 1/4 cups buttermilk
1 teaspoon Worcestershire
    sauce

■ In a skillet cook the bacon until crisp. Drain on paper towels. In a bowl combine the flour, cornmeal, salt, baking soda, and baking powder. Add the cheese and dill and stir to combine. In a large bowl stir together the shortening and sugar. Add the eggs and mix well. Stir in the buttermilk and Worcestershire sauce. Add the flour mixture and the bacon, and stir just until combined. Divide the batter among 3 greased 5x3x2-inch loaf pans. Bake at 350° for 40 to 50 minutes or until a toothpick inserted in the center comes out clean.

CARROT BREAD
1 loaf

1 cup sugar	1/2 cup chopped walnuts
3/4 cup oil	1 teaspoon baking soda
2 eggs	1 1/2 cups all-purpose flour
1/4 teaspoon salt	1/2 teaspoon cinnamon
1/2 cup grated carrots	1/2 teaspoon nutmeg

■ In a large bowl combine the sugar and oil. Add the eggs and salt. Stir in the carrots and walnuts. Sift the dry ingredients together and add to the carrot mixture. Stir the batter until just combined. Pour into a greased 9x3-inch loaf pan. Bake at 350° for 1 hour.

EGGNOG BREAD
1 loaf

3 cups all-purpose flour	1 1/2 cups eggnog
3/4 cup sugar	1 egg, beaten
1 tablespoon baking powder	1/4 cup melted butter
1 teaspoon salt	3/4 cup chopped walnuts
1/2 teaspoon nutmeg	3/4 cup chopped candied fruit

■ In a large bowl sift together the flour, sugar, baking powder, salt and nutmeg. In a separate bowl combine the eggnog, egg, and butter. Stir into the dry ingredients. Stir in the walnuts and candied fruit. Pour into a greased 9x5x2-inch loaf pan. Bake at 350° for 1 hour or until a wooden toothpick inserted in the center comes out clean.

LEMON BREAD
1 loaf

3/4 cup (1 1/2 sticks) butter	3/4 cup buttermilk
1 1/2 cups sugar	Grated rind of 1 lemon
3 eggs	3/4 cup chopped pecans
2 1/4 cups all-purpose flour	Juice of 2 lemons
1/4 teaspoon salt	3/4 cup confectioners' sugar
1/4 teaspoon baking soda	

■ In a large bowl cream together the butter and sugar. Beat in the eggs one at a time. Combine the dry ingredients and add to the creamed mixture alternately with the buttermilk. Stir in the grated lemon rind and nuts. Spoon into a greased and floured 9x5x3-inch loaf pan. Bake at 325° for 1 hour and 20 minutes. While the loaf is baking, prepare a glaze by combining the lemon juice and confectioners' sugar. Let stand to allow the sugar to dissolve. After removing the loaf from the pan, pierce the top with a toothpick in a number of places and spoon the glaze over the loaf.

OATMEAL MOLASSES BREAD
2 loaves

1 cup old-fashioned rolled oats	1¼ cups buttermilk
1 cup whole wheat flour	½ cup raisins
1 cup all-purpose flour	1 tablespoon cold unsalted butter
1 teaspoon salt	2 tablespoons brown sugar
1 teaspoon baking soda	2 tablespoons all-purpose flour
1 teaspoon baking powder	1 teaspoon cinnamon
¼ cup sugar	3 tablespoons old-fashioned rolled oats
1 large egg, beaten lightly	
⅓ cup dark molasses	

■ In a bowl combine the rolled oats, flours, salt, baking soda, and baking powder. In a large bowl stir together the sugar, egg, and molasses. Add the buttermilk and blend well. Add the flour mixture and raisins, and stir until just combined. Divide the batter between 2 greased 7x3x2-inch loaf pans. In a small bowl blend together the butter, brown sugar, 2 tablespoons of flour, the cinnamon, and 3 tablespoons of oats until crumbly. Sprinkle over the batter. Bake at 350° for 45 to 50 minutes.

ORANGE SLICE NUT BREAD
1 loaf

1 cup candied orange slices, finely chopped	2½ cups sifted all-purpose flour
1 tablespoon sugar	2 teaspoons baking powder
¼ cup butter	½ teaspoon baking soda
½ cup sugar	½ teaspoon salt
1 egg	½ cup chopped nuts
½ cup mashed banana	1 cup milk

■ Sprinkle the chopped orange slices with 1 tablespoon of sugar to prevent the pieces from sticking together. Cream the butter with ½ cup of sugar, add the egg and banana and mix well. Sift together the dry ingredients and add the nuts and orange slices. Add alternately with the milk to the creamed mixture. Pour into a greased and floured 8x4x3-inch loaf pan. Bake at 350° for 65 minutes or until done. Let stand overnight before slicing.

PEANUT BUTTER BREAD
1 loaf

2½ cups all-purpose flour	¾ cup sugar
4 teaspoons baking powder	1 teaspoon vanilla extract
½ teaspoon salt	1 egg
¾ cup peanut butter	1¾ cups milk

■ Sift together the dry ingredients. In a large bowl combine the peanut butter, sugar, and vanilla and beat until well blended. Add the egg. Gradually add the milk until well blended and then add the flour mixture. Spoon the batter into a greased 9x5-inch loaf pan. Bake at 350° for 1 hour.

SALT RISING BREAD
2 loaves

1 cup milk	1 teaspoon salt
2 tablespoons cornmeal	1 tablespoon sugar
1 teaspoon salt	2 tablespoons shortening
1 tablespoon sugar	5¼ cups sifted all-purpose
1 cup lukewarm water	flour

■ In a saucepan scald the milk and cool to lukewarm. Add the cornmeal, 1 teaspoon of salt, and 1 tablespoon of sugar. Pour into a fruit jar or pitcher, cover, and place in a pan of hot water (120°). Let stand for 6 to 7 hours or until signs of fermentation appear. Add the lukewarm water, 1 teaspoon of salt, 1 tablespoon of sugar, the shortening, and 2 cups of flour. Beat thoroughly, cover, and place in a pan of hot water (120°). Let rise until very light, then add the remaining flour gradually until the dough is stiff enough to be kneaded. Knead for 15 to 20 minutes and shape into 2 loaves. Place in greased bread pans and brush the tops with melted shortening. Cover and let rise until very light, more than doubled. Bake at 375° for 10 minutes, reduce to 350° and bake 25 to 30 minutes longer.

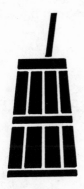

BUTTERY YEAST ROLLS
5 to 6 dozen rolls

¾ cup butter, softened
1 cup boiling water
2 teaspoons salt
½ cup sugar
2 ¼-ounce packages active
   dry yeast

½ cup warm water (110° to
   115°)
2 eggs, beaten
¾ cup icy cold water
6½ to 7½ cups all-purpose
   flour

■ In a large bowl combine the butter, boiling water, salt, and sugar until thoroughly blended. Cool to warm. In a separate bowl soften the yeast in the warm water. Blend in the eggs and cold water. Beat into the butter mixture. Add 3 cups of flour, ½ cup at a time, beating vigorously after each addition until the batter is smooth. Add enough of the remaining flour to make a soft dough that does not stick to the sides of the bowl. Turn the dough out onto a lightly floured surface; set aside to rest for 5 to 10 minutes. Knead until satiny and smooth. Form into a ball and put into a greased deep bowl. Turn the dough until the greased side is on top. Cover tightly and refrigerate overnight or for several days.

Remove the dough and punch down. Brush the top with oil. Cover and let rise in a warm place until doubled, about 1 to 2½ hours. Shape as desired, place on greased baking sheets, and let rise again until light. Bake at 425° for 12 to 15 minutes.

BUTTERMILK YEAST ROLLS
3 dozen rolls

4 cups all-purpose flour
¼ cup sugar
1 teaspoon baking powder
1 teaspoon salt
¼ teaspoon baking soda
1 cup shortening

1 ¼-ounce package active dry
   yeast
¼ cup warm water (110° to
   115°)
1 teaspoon sugar
1 cup buttermilk

■ In a large mixing bowl combine the flour, sugar, baking powder, salt, and baking soda. Blend the shortening into the dry ingredients. Dissolve the yeast in the warm water to which 1 teaspoon of sugar has been added. Set aside to foam. Add the buttermilk and yeast to the flour mixture and mix well. Cover and refrigerate until chilled, several hours or overnight.

Turn the dough out onto a floured board and knead until smooth. Roll to about ½-inch thickness. Shape as desired and place on a greased baking sheet. Set aside to rise in a warm place for about 2 hours or until doubled in bulk. Bake at 425° until evenly browned.

QUICK SPOON ROLLS
18 rolls

1 ¼-ounce package active dry yeast
¼ cup lukewarm water (110° to 115°)
½ cup sugar
⅓ cup shortening
1 teaspoon salt
¾ cup milk, scalded
½ cup water
1 egg
3½ cups sifted all-purpose flour

■ Dissolve the yeast in the warm water and set aside. In a large bowl combine the sugar, shortening, salt, and hot milk. Cool to lukewarm by adding the water. Blend in the egg and the dissolved yeast. Add the flour and mix until well blended. Place in a greased bowl and turn until the greased side is up. Cover and let rise for 45 to 60 minutes, until doubled in bulk. Stir down the dough and spoon into well-greased muffin cups, filling half full. Let rise for about 45 minutes, until the batter has risen to the edge of the muffin cups and is rounded in the center. Bake at 400° for 15 to 20 minutes.

SWEET POTATO ROLLS
32 rolls

1 ¼-ounce package active dry yeast	⅔ cup shortening
1½ cups warm water (105° to 115°)	2 eggs
	1 cup lukewarm mashed sweet potatoes
⅓ cup sugar	7 to 7½ cups all-purpose flour
1¼ teaspoons salt	Soft margarine or butter

■ In a large bowl dissolve the yeast in warm water. Stir in the sugar, salt, shortening, eggs, sweet potatoes and half of the flour. Add the remaining flour until the dough is easy to handle. Turn the dough onto a lightly floured board and knead until smooth and elastic, about 5 minutes. Place in a greased bowl, and turn until the greased side is up. Cover the bowl with plastic wrap and refrigerate.

Two hours before baking, divide the dough in half. Roll each half into a 16-inch circle, about ¼-inch thick. Spread with margarine. Cut each circle into 16 wedges. Beginning at the rounded edge, roll each triangle up. Place with the point underneath on a baking sheet. Set aside to rise for about 1 hour. Bake at 400° for 15 to 20 minutes.

BUTTERY EGG BREAD
3 loaves

2 ¼-ounce packages active dry yeast	½ cup sugar
½ cup warm water (110° to 115°)	2½ teaspoons salt
	8 cups all-purpose flour
1½ cups milk	1 tablespoon butter, melted
½ cup butter, cut into 6 pieces	1 egg yolk
3 eggs, beaten	2 teaspoons water
	2 teaspoons poppy seeds

■ Dissolve the yeast in the warm water and set aside. In a small saucepan combine the milk and butter. Cook over low heat, stirring until the butter melts. In a large bowl, combine the eggs, sugar, salt, and yeast mixture, then stir in the milk mixture. Beat in 7½ cups of flour, about 2 cups at a time. Turn the dough out onto a floured surface and knead until smooth and elastic, about 5 to 8 minutes, adding the remaining ½ cup of flour as needed. Place in a greased bowl and turn until the greased side is up. Cover and let rise for 1½ hours, until doubled in bulk.

Punch down and turn out onto a floured surface. Let rest for 30 minutes. Knead 3 or 4 times. Divide the dough into thirds, and shape each third into a loaf. Place the loaves in greased bread pans and brush the tops with melted butter. Cover and let rise for 30 minutes or until doubled in bulk.

Combine the egg yolk and water in a small bowl and stir well. Brush the mixture over the loaves. Sprinkle with poppy seeds. Bake at 350° for 25 to 30 minutes or until the loaves sound hollow when tapped.

HONEY WHEAT BREAD
2 loaves

1½ cups water	2 tablespoons sugar
½ cup honey	2 teaspoons salt
1 cup cream-style cottage cheese	5½ to 6 cups all-purpose flour
¼ cup butter	1 cup whole wheat flour
1 egg, beaten	
2 ¼-ounce packages active dry yeast	

■ In a small saucepan combine the water, honey, cottage cheese, and butter. Heat until very warm (120° to 130°). In a large bowl combine the egg, yeast, sugar, and salt, mixing well. Add the cottage cheese mixture, 3 cups of flour, and the whole wheat flour. Beat at medium speed of an electric mixer for 2 minutes. Gradually stir in enough remaining flour to make a soft dough. Turn the dough out onto a well-floured surface and knead for about 5 minutes until smooth and elastic. Place in a well-greased bowl and turn until the greased side is up. Cover and let rise for about 1 hour. Punch down and let rest for 5 minutes. Divide the dough in half, and shape each half into a loaf. Place each loaf in a greased loaf pan. Cover and let rise for 1 hour or until doubled in bulk. Bake at 350° for 45 minutes or until the loaf sounds hollow when tapped.

ONION DILL BREAD
1 loaf

1½ cups all-purpose flour	1 teaspoon salt
1 ¼-ounce package active dry yeast	2 tablespoons butter, cut up
1 medium onion, minced	1 egg
1 stalk fresh dill, minced	2 cups all-purpose flour
1¼ cups milk	
2 tablespoons sugar	

■ In a large bowl combine 1½ cups of flour with the yeast.
Set aside. Combine the onion, dill, and milk. In a saucepan
combine the milk mixture, sugar, salt, and butter pieces.
Heat, stirring constantly to melt the butter, until just
warm (110° to 115°). Add the milk mixture and the egg to
the flour and beat until thoroughly combined. Gradually
stir in the remaining 2 cups of flour, adding additional
flour if necessary to make a dough of medium stiffness.
Turn the dough out on a lightly floured surface and knead
for about 10 minutes. Place in a greased bowl and turn until the greased side is up. Cover and let rise until double in
bulk, about 30 minutes. Punch down and shape into a loaf.
Place in a greased bread pan. Cover and let rise until the
dough fills the pan. Bake at 350° for 35 to 40 minutes.

TOMATO BREAD
2 loaves

2 cups tomato juice	1 ¼-ounce package active dry yeast
2 tablespoons butter	
3 tablespoons honey	¼ cup warm water (110° to 115°)
1 teaspoon salt	
¼ cup catsup	6½ cups all-purpose flour

■ Heat the tomato juice and butter in a saucepan until the butter melts. Stir in the honey, salt, and catsup. Cool to lukewarm. Dissolve the yeast in ¼ cup of warm water in a large mixer bowl. Add the tomato mixture and 3 cups of flour. Beat at medium speed for 2 minutes. Stir in enough of the remaining flour to make a medium dough. Knead on a floured surface until smooth and elastic. Place in a greased bowl, turning to grease the surface of the dough. Let the dough rise, covered, in a warm place until doubled in bulk. Divide into 2 portions. Let the dough rest for 10 minutes. Shape into loaves and place in 2 greased loaf pans. Let the dough rise until nearly doubled in bulk. Bake at 425° for 25 minutes or until the loaves test done.

White bread
2 loaves

1 ¼-ounce package active dry yeast	1½ teaspoons salt
1 teaspoon sugar	2 tablespoons shortening
¼ cup lukewarm water (110° to 115°)	2 tablespoons sugar
	2 cups milk, scalded
	6 cups sifted all-purpose flour

■ Dissolve the yeast and 1 teaspoon of sugar in the warm water and set aside. In a large bowl combine the salt, shortening, 2 tablespoons of sugar, and milk. Cool to lukewarm. Add the yeast mixture and 3 cups of flour. Beat well. Add enough more flour to make a soft dough. Place the remaining flour on a board and turn the dough out. Knead until smooth and elastic. Place in a greased bowl and turn until the greased side is up. Cover and let rise until doubled in bulk. Punch down and let rise a second time if desired. Cut the dough in half and round each half into a ball. Cover and let stand for 10 minutes. Shape into loaves and place in greased bread pans. Grease the tops of the loaves, cover with a cloth, and let rise until doubled in bulk. Bake at 400° for 10 minutes, reduce to 375°, and bake 35 to 40 minutes longer.

Condiments

■ ■ ■ ■ ■ ■ ■ ■ ■ ■

CRISP SWEET BREAD AND BUTTER PICKLES

4 quarts medium cucumbers,
   sliced
6 medium white onions,
   sliced
2 green peppers, chopped
3 cups cider vinegar

3 cloves garlic
5 cups sugar
1/3 cup coarse salt
1 1/2 teaspoons turmeric
1 1/2 teaspoons mustard seed

■ Make a hot brine out of the vinegar and spices and pour over the vegetables. Let cool. Drain and put the vegetables into sterile jars. Boil the vinegar and spices once again and pour over the vegetables in jars. Seal and let stand a few days.

CRISP SWEET GREEN TOMATO PICKLES
8 pints

8 pounds green tomatoes
2 cups lime (from builders supply)
2 gallons water
9 cups sugar

5 to 8 cups apple cider vinegar
1 tablespoon salt
10 drops green food color (optional)

■ Cut the tomatoes into ½-inch slices. Combine the lime and water and pour over the tomatoes. Let stand for 24 hours. Rinse well and soak in cold water for 2 hours. Mix the sugar, vinegar, salt and food coloring. Drain the tomatoes and add to the sugar mixture. Soak the tomatoes in this mixture overnight. Bring to a boil and boil for 40 minutes. Pour into sterilized jars and seal at once.

WATERMELON RIND PICKLES
4 quarts

7 pounds watermelon rind
1 tablespoon slaked lime
1 gallon water

4 pounds sugar
1 pint vinegar
2 sticks cinnamon

■ Peel and cut the rind in ½-inch thick slices. Soak overnight in a mixture of the lime and water. Wash several times and place in a large saucepan or kettle. Cover with clear water and cook until tender. Drain. Boil the sugar, vinegar, and cinnamon together, cool, and then pour over the rind. Let the mixture stand overnight. Bring to a boil and boil until the rind is transparent. Pack the fruit into jars and pour in the hot syrup. Seal at once.

EASY APPLE BUTTER

5 cups applesauce
7 cups sugar
1/4 cup vinegar

1 teaspoon cinnamon or
  allspice

■ In a heavy saucepan combine all of the ingredients and bring to a boil on high heat. Reduce the heat and boil for 15 minutes, stirring occasionally. Pour into sterilized jars and seal at once.

MAPLE BUTTER
1 1/4 cups

1 cup butter, softened
1/4 cup maple or maple-
  flavored syrup

1/2 teaspoon ground cinnamon

■ In a small bowl combine all of the ingredients until blended.

BANANA-PECAN BUTTER
8 half-pint jars

3 cups crushed ripe
  bananas
1 teaspoon grated lemon
  peel
1/4 cup lemon juice
6 1/2 cups sugar

1/2 teaspoon butter or
  margarine
1 bottle liquid fruit pectin
1 cup pecans, chopped

■ In a large heavy saucepan combine the bananas, lemon peel and juice, sugar and butter and blend thoroughly. Bring to a boil and boil for 2 minutes, stirring constantly. Remove from the heat and stir in the pectin and chopped pecans. Spoon into hot sterilized jars and seal.

ORANGE BUTTER
1 cup

½ cup butter	2 tablespoons grated orange
1 3-ounce package cream	rind
cheese	1 tablespoon frozen orange
⅓ cup confectioners' sugar	juice concentrate

■ Bring the butter and cream cheese to room temperature. Beat all of the ingredients until smooth.

MULLED CIDER SYRUP
1¼ cups

2 cups apple cider	½ teaspoon ground cinnamon
¼ cup granulated sugar	¼ teaspoon ground cloves
¼ cup packed light brown	¼ teaspoon ground nutmeg
sugar	
½ cup apple jelly	

■ In a 1-quart saucepan combine the cider and sugars. Cook, without stirring, over medium heat until the sugars dissolve. Stir in the jelly, cinnamon, cloves and nutmeg and heat to boiling. Reduce the heat to low and simmer, stirring until the jelly melts. Remove from the heat to cool slightly. Serve warm.

APPLE OR CRABAPPLE JELLY

■ Cut unpared, uncored apples into eighths. In a large saucepan cover the apples with water and simmer until soft. Strain through a jelly bag and measure the juice. Bring the juice to a boil, skim, and add ¾ cup of sugar for each cup of juice. Stir until the sugar dissolves and cook until the syrup runs off the spoon in a sheet. Flavor with oil of cinnamon and color with red coloring if desired. Pour into hot sterilized glasses and seal at once.

GRAPE JELLY

■ Wash and stem the grapes. Crush the grapes, add small amount of water and boil for 15 minutes. Strain through a jelly bag. Measure the juice and bring to the boiling point. For each cup of juice add ¾ cup of sugar. Boil rapidly to the jelly stage. Pour into sterilized glasses.

HOT PEPPER JELLY

1 large bell pepper
1½ cups cider vinegar
6½ cups sugar
1 teaspoon salt

½ cup hot pepper
1 bottle Certo
Green or red food coloring

■ Remove the seeds and membrane from the bell pepper and grind to make ¾ cup of pulp and juice. Add the vinegar, sugar, salt and hot peppers (ground and seeded). Bring to a rolling boil and add the Certo. Bring to a boil again, stirring constantly for 1 minute. Add 8 to 10 drops of food coloring. Strain if desired. Pour into sterilized jars and seal at once.

MINT JELLY

1 cup mint leaves (packed
   tightly)
1 cup boiling water

1 cup apple juice
¾ cup sugar
Green food coloring

■ Pour boiling water over the mint leaves. Steep for 1 hour. Press the juice from the leaves. Add 2 tablespoons of this extract to the apple juice and sugar and boil rapidly to the jelly stage. Tint with green food coloring. Pour into sterilized glasses and seal at once.

CARROT JAM

5 pounds carrots
Juice of 6 lemons

6 cups of sugar

■ Wash, pare, and grate the carrots. Add the lemon juice and sugar and cook slowly until thick. Pour into sterilized jars and seal at once.

DAMSON PLUM JAM

4 quarts damson plums
1 quart cold water

Sugar

■ Wash the plums, remove the seeds, add the water and cook the fruit until soft. Measure and add two-thirds as much sugar as fruit. Stir the mixture over low heat until the sugar is dissolved. Boil rapidly until the mixture is thick and clear. The flavor of the plums should be practically unchanged and the color rich and sparkling red. Pour into sterilized jars and seal at once.

PEACHY ORANGE JAM
5 half-pint jars

3 large juicy oranges
1 lemon
6 cups confectioners' sugar

3 pounds (about 12) medium firm peaches

■ Grate the orange and lemon rinds. Squeeze the juices and remove the seeds. Do not strain. In a large heavy kettle combine the rinds and juices. Peel and chop the peaches into the citrus juices. Stir in the sugar and bring to a boil over medium heat, stirring often. Reduce the heat and simmer slowly until thickened, about 35 to 40 minutes. Stir frequently, do not cover. Pour into hot sterilized jars and seal at once.

Rhubarb-Strawberry Jam

2 pounds rhubarb

6 cups sugar
2 pounds strawberries

■ Wash the fruit and cut the rhubarb into ½-inch pieces. Cover the rhubarb with half of the sugar and let stand for 1 to 2 hours. Crush the berries, mix with the remaining sugar, and combine with the rhubarb. Heat the mixture over low heat until the sugar is dissolved, then boil rapidly, stirring frequently to prevent burning. Cook until thick. Pour into sterilized jars and seal at once.

Tomato Jam

5 pounds ripe tomatoes
5 cups brown sugar
2½ cups vinegar
1 tablespoon whole cloves

1 tablespoon allspice
1 stick cinnamon
3 cups seedless raisins,
chopped

■ Peel and cut the tomatoes into pieces. Add the sugar and vinegar and spices tied in a cheesecloth. Boil slowly for 2 hours. Add the raisins and boil 1 hour longer. Remove the spices, pour into sterilized jars and seal at once.

Carrot and Orange Marmalade

6 oranges
4 lemons
4 cups water

6 cups carrots
5 cups sugar

■ Chop the peel of all the oranges and two lemons. Soak the peel in the 4 cups of water overnight and drain. Cut the oranges into small pieces, and dice the carrots. Add the peel and oranges to the carrots and cook until tender in as little water as possible. Add the sugar and water in which the peels were soaked and cook until thick and clear. Add the lemon juice and cook for 5 minutes. Pour into sterilized jars and seal at once.

ZUCCHINI MARMALADE
6 half-pint jars

6 cups peeled and thinly
  sliced zucchini
Juice of 2 lemons
1 teaspoon grated lemon
  peel
1½ cups drained, crushed
  pineapple

1 1¾-ounce package fruit
  pectin
5 cups sugar
2 tablespoons finely chopped
  crystallized ginger

■ In a large saucepan combine the zucchini, lemon juice, lemon peel, and pineapple, and bring to a boil. Reduce the heat and simmer uncovered until zucchini is tender, about 15 minutes. Add the fruit pectin and mix well. Bring to a boil and stir in the sugar and ginger. Boil for 1 minute, stirring constantly. Remove from the heat and stir for 5 minutes, skimming off any foam. Ladle into hot sterilized jars and seal at once.

TOMATO PRESERVES

2 cups peeled and chopped
  green or red tomatoes
2 cups sugar

1 lemon
1 stick cinnamon

■ Combine the tomatoes and sugar and let stand for 12 hours. Drain and bring the juice to a boil. Boil the juice until thick and add the tomatoes, lemon juice, grated lemon rind, and cinnamon. Cook until thick. Pour into sterilized jars and seal at once.

DRIED APRICOT-PINEAPPLE PRESERVES
Six 6-ounce glasses

2 cups dried apricots
2½ cups water
2 cups canned crushed
  pineapple

½ lemon, sliced
4 cups sugar

■ Rinse the apricots and simmer them in water until tender. Mash the apricots and add the remaining ingredients. Simmer, stirring frequently, until thick and clear. Pour into sterilized jars and seal at once.

TOMATO CATSUP
2 pints

1½ teaspoons whole cloves
1½ teaspoons broken stick
  cinnamon
1 teaspoon celery seed
1 cup white vinegar

8 pounds ripe tomatoes
1 tablespoon chopped onion
¼ teaspoon red pepper
1 cup sugar
4 teaspoons salt

■ In a saucepan combine the spices and vinegar, and bring to a boil. Remove from the heat and set aside. Peel the tomatoes and place in a large saucepan or kettle. Add the onion and red pepper and bring to a boil. Cook for 15 minutes, stirring occasionally. Strain the tomatoes through a coarse sieve, add the sugar, and bring to a boil. Reduce the heat to a simmer and cook until the mixture has reduced to half, about 45 to 60 minutes. Strain the vinegar and spices into the tomatoes and discard the spices. Add the salt. Simmer all together until the mixture is the desired consistency. Pour into hot sterilized jars and seal at once.

CORN RELISH

7 cups

1 medium onion,
    finely chopped
2 tablespoons oil
2 teaspoons turmeric
½ cup water
2 tablespoons cornstarch
1 24-ounce package frozen
    whole-kernel corn
1 small head green cabbage,
    coarsely chopped

1 medium red pepper,
    coarsely chopped
1 cup sugar
1 cup white vinegar
2 teaspoons salt
1 teaspoon dry mustard
½ teaspoon celery seed

■ In a Dutch oven over medium heat sauté the onion in hot oil until tender, stirring occasionally. Stir in the turmeric and cook for 1 minute. Combine the cornstarch and water. Stir into the onions, and then add the remaining ingredients and mix well. Bring the relish to a boil over medium high heat, and stir until the relish thickens slightly, boiling for 1 minute. Place the relish in a serving dish and chill for several hours.

PEPPER RELISH

2 cups chopped red bell
    peppers
2 cups chopped green bell
    peppers
2 cups chopped onions

Salt
2 cups chopped celery
2¼ tablespoons salt
1⅓ cups sugar
2⅓ cups vinegar

■ Cover the vegetables with boiling water and simmer for 10 or 15 minutes. Drain well. Add the remaining ingredients and boil 15 to 30 minutes. Pour into sterilized jars and seal at once.

YELLOW SQUASH RELISH

8 cups thinly sliced yellow
  squash
2 cups thinly sliced onions
2 red bell peppers, sliced
2 green bell peppers, sliced

3 cups sugar
2 cups white vinegar
2 teaspoons mustard seed
2 teaspoons celery seed

■ Combine the vegetables and salt to taste. Let stand for 2 hours and drain. In a large pot combine the sugar, vinegar, and spices and bring to a boil. Add the vegetables, bring to a boil and boil for 5 minutes. Pour into hot jars and seal at once.

APPLE PICKLES
10 pints

18 large apples, peeled
12 large onions
 1 strong pepper
10 sweet peppers
   (5 red, 5 green)

3 pints vinegar
3 cups sugar

■ Chop the apples, onions, and peppers into small pieces and mix together. In a large saucepan or kettle bring all of the ingredients to a boil. Pour into sterilized jars and seal at once.

BEET PICKLES

 1 gallon beets
 2 cups sugar
3½ cups vinegar

Dash cinnamon
1 tablespoon allspice
1½ cups water

■ Peel the beets by heating and slipping off the skin. Add the remaining ingredients and simmer all together for 15 minutes. Pour into sterilized jars and seal at once.

TOMATO BARBECUE SAUCE
1 quart

4 16-ounce cans tomatoes
1 cup chopped onion
2 cloves garlic, finely
 minced
1 cup brown sugar
4 tablespoons butter

1 cup chili sauce
¼ cup Worcestershire sauce
¼ cup lemon juice
 Salt to taste
1 teaspoon dry mustard
 Dash nutmeg, optional

■ Combine all of the ingredients in a large saucepan and bring to a boil. Reduce the heat and simmer uncovered for about 2 hours, stirring frequently, until thickened. Adjust the seasonings to taste. Store covered in the refrigerator.

CREAMY GRAVY

¼ cup all-purpose flour
 Salt and pepper to taste
¼ cup pan drippings

1 cup light cream
1 cup chicken stock

■ Stir the flour, salt and pepper into the hot pan drippings, then add the cream and stock, stirring constantly until the gravy begins to thicken.

GIBLET GRAVY

¼ cup butter
¼ cup all-purpose flour
3 cups chicken stock

Salt and pepper to taste
Cooked giblets, finely chopped

■ In a small skillet melt the butter over medium heat and stir in the flour. Cook for about 2 minutes, then add the stock, salt and pepper, and cook for 5 more minutes, stirring constantly. Add the giblets and cook 1 more minute.

HOMEMADE MUSTARD
1½ cups

4 tablespoons dry mustard
3 tablespoons sugar
2 eggs, whipped

¾ cup cider vinegar
2 tablespoons olive oil

■ Thoroughly mix the mustard and sugar. Slowly add the eggs. Bring the vinegar almost to a boil. Pour the vinegar into the mustard mixture and return to heat until thickened. Cool, and add the olive oil.

HORSERADISH SAUCE
1 cup

½ cup heavy cream
4 tablespoons horseradish, freshly grated
Few drops onion juice

Dash cayenne pepper
1½ tablespoons cider vinegar

■ Whip the cream and fold the remaining ingredients into it. Serve chilled.

Hot PEPPER SAUCE
2 pints

8 to 10 bell peppers
8 cayenne peppers
1 cup sugar

1 cup water
2 cups dark vinegar

■ Remove the core and seeds from the bell peppers. Cut into 1-inch slices and place in sterile jars with whole cayenne peppers. In a large saucepan bring the sugar, water, and vinegar to a hard rolling boil, stirring constantly. Boil for 3 minutes. Pour the liquid over the peppers and seal at once.

Allow 4 to 6 weeks before using. When ready to use, refrigerate and chill thoroughly. This keeps them crisp. The juice is excellent over any type of greens and the peppers are great to eat along with your greens, white beans and cornbread, or pone. When cooking white beans or turnip greens, to add a little more flavor throw in 1 or 2 fresh cayenne peppers. It enhances the flavor.

White CHEESE SAUCE
1 to 1½ cups

2 tablespoons butter
2 tablespoons all-purpose
flour
¼ teaspoon salt

⅛ teaspoon pepper
1 cup milk
½ to 1 cup grated Cheddar
cheese

■ In a saucepan over low heat melt the butter. Blend in the flour, salt, and pepper. Cook over low heat, stirring constantly, until the mixture is smooth and bubbly. Remove from heat and stir in the milk. Heat to boiling, stirring constantly. Boil and stir for 1 minute. Add the cheese, reduce the heat to low, and stir until the cheese melts and the sauce is smooth.

TARTAR SAUCE
1⅔ cups

1 cup mayonnaise
⅓ cup chopped dill pickle
⅓ cup chopped onion

1½ teaspoons chopped capers
½ teaspoon mustard
½ teaspoon lemon juice

■ Combine all of the ingredients and refrigerate an hour before serving with seafood.

HOT FUDGE SAUCE
2 cups

4 squares unsweetened
  chocolate
2 tablespoons butter
¾ cup boiling water

2 cups sugar
3 tablespoons corn syrup
2 tablespoons vanilla extract

■ Chop the chocolate coarsely and heat with butter and boiling water in a large heavy saucepan over low heat, stirring constantly until the chocolate is melted. Add the sugar and corn syrup. Bring the mixture slowly to boiling, reduce the heat and simmer gently for 8 minutes. Watch carefully but do not stir. Add the vanilla. Serve while warm.

PRALINE SAUCE
2 cups

1 cup finely chopped pecans
½ cup butter

½ cup dark brown sugar
¾ cup water
2 tablespoons cornstarch

■ In a saucepan over medium-low heat, brown the pecans in hot butter. Stir in the brown sugar. Stir together the water and cornstarch until smooth. Stir into the pecan mixture and cook over medium-high heat, stirring constantly, until the mixture thickens slightly and boils.

HOT BUTTERSCOTCH SAUCE

1 cup light brown sugar   *2 tablespoons light corn syrup*
¼ cup half-and-half
2 tablespoons butter

■ In a heavy saucepan over medium heat, heat all of the ingredients to boiling, stirring frequently. Serve the sauce hot.

Desserts
■ ■ ■ ■ ■ ■ ■

Buttermilk pound cake

1 cup butter, softened
2 cups sugar
4 eggs
3 cups all-purpose flour
½ teaspoon baking soda

¼ teaspoon salt
1 cup buttermilk
1 teaspoon vanilla extract
1 teaspoon lemon extract

■ In a large bowl cream the butter, gradually adding the sugar. Beat at medium speed of an electric mixer until well-blended. Add the eggs, one at a time, beating after each addition. In a separate bowl combine the flour, baking soda and salt. Add to the creamed mixture alternately with the buttermilk, beginning and ending with the flour mixture. Stir in the flavorings. Pour into a greased and floured 10-inch tube pan. Bake at 325° for 1 hour or until a wooden toothpick inserted in the center comes out clean. Cool in the pan for 10 minutes, then remove from the pan and cool completely on a rack.

CARROT CAKE

4 eggs
1½ cups oil
2 cups all-purpose flour
2 cups sugar
2 teaspoons baking powder
2 teaspoons baking soda
3 teaspoons cinnamon
1 teaspoon salt
3 cups packed grated raw
    carrots

½ cup chopped black walnuts
1 pound confectioners' sugar
½ cup butter, softened
1 8-ounce package cream
    cheese
½ cup chopped black walnuts
    (optional)

■ In a large bowl beat together the eggs and oil. Combine the dry ingredients and add to the egg and oil mixture. Beat well. Add the carrots and walnuts and blend well. Pour into 3 greased 9-inch layer pans. Bake at 350° for 25 minutes. Blend together the remaining ingredients and spread on the cake. Refrigerate the cake.

CHOCOLATE LOAF CAKE

¾ cup butter, room
    temperature
1 cup packed dark brown
    sugar
1 cup sugar
1 teaspoon vanilla extract
2 eggs

1 cup coarsely chopped
    pecans
1¾ cups all-purpose flour
1 teaspoon baking powder
½ teaspoon baking soda
½ cup cocoa
⅔ cup buttermilk

■ Cream the butter. Gradually add the sugar and vanilla, beating well. Add the eggs, one at a time. Beat for 2 minutes. Coat the nuts with 1 tablespoon of flour, and set aside. Combine the remaining dry ingredients and add to the creamed mixture alternately with the buttermilk, mixing well after each addition. Add the nuts. Pour into a greased and floured 9x5-inch loaf pan. Bake at 350° for 1 hour or until the cake tests done.

GINGERBREAD WITH LEMON SAUCE

1½ cups unsifted all-purpose
 flour
1½ teaspoons baking soda
 ¼ teaspoon salt
 ¼ teaspoon ground
  cinnamon
 ½ teaspoon ground ginger
 ¼ teaspoon ground cloves
 1 egg
 1 cup light molasses

½ cup butter, melted
½ cup hot water
½ cup sugar
 2 tablespoons cornstarch
 1 cup water
 ¼ cup butter
 2 teaspoons grated lemon
  peel
 Dash salt
 ¼ cup lemon juice

■ Sift together the flour, baking soda, salt, and spices. In a large bowl beat the egg, molasses, butter and hot water with an electric mixer until well blended. Gradually beat in the flour mixture, beating until smooth. Pour into an 8-inch cake pan and bake at 375° for 25 minutes or until the cake tests done.

  In a small saucepan combine the sugar and cornstarch. Add 1 cup of water, stirring until smooth. Bring the mixture to a boil, stirring constantly. Reduce the heat to a simmer, and stir until the mixture is thickened and translucent. Remove from the heat and stir in the remaining ingredients. Pour over the gingerbread.

MOCHA CAKE

¾ cup sugar
 1 cup sifted all-purpose flour
 2 teaspoons baking powder
⅛ teaspoon salt
 1 ounce unsweetened
  chocolate
 2 tablespoons butter

½ cup milk
 1 teaspoon vanilla extract
½ cup brown sugar
½ cup sugar
 4 tablespoons cocoa
 1 cup cold, strong coffee

■ Sift together the sugar, flour, baking soda, and salt. In a double boiler or heavy saucepan melt the chocolate with the butter. Add to the flour mixture and blend well. Combine the milk and vanilla, and add to the chocolate mixture. Pour into a greased 8-inch pan. Combine the brown sugar, sugar, and cocoa and sprinkle over the batter. Pour the coffee over the top. Bake at 350° for 40 minutes.

OLD-FASHIONED JAM CAKE

¾ cup shortening
 2 cups sugar
 6 eggs, separated and beaten
 2 cups blackberry jam
 4 cups all-purpose flour
½ teaspoon salt
 2 teaspoons soda, mixed with
  buttermilk
 2 teaspoons cinnamon
 2 teaspoons allspice
 2 teaspoons cloves

 1 cup buttermilk
1½ cups raisins
 1 cup nuts, chopped
1½ tablespoons all-purpose
  flour
 2 cups sugar
 2 cups evaporated milk
1½ cups raisins
1½ cups nuts, chopped
 2 cups coconut

■ Cream together the sugar and shortening. Add the beaten egg yolks, then the jam. Sift together the dry ingredients and add alternately with the milk, beating well after each addition. Add the raisins and nuts, then fold in the beaten egg whites. Pour into three 9-inch pans. Bake at 350° for 45 minutes or until the cake tests done.

Combine the flour and sugar, then add the milk. Mix all of the ingredients together and cook until thick. Set aside until cold. Spread between the layers of cake and outside the cake.

OLD-FASHIONED PRUNE CAKE

1 cup light brown sugar
¾ cup shortening
3 tablespoons sour cream
3 eggs
2 cups all-purpose flour, sifted
1 teaspoon soda
1 teaspoon allspice
2 teaspoons cinnamon

1 cup prunes, cooked and chopped
2 eggs
1 cup light brown sugar
2 tablespoons margarine
½ cup heavy cream
1 cup prunes, cooked and chopped

■ Blend together 1 cup of brown sugar, the shortening, sour cream, and 3 eggs. Add the dry ingredients, blend well, then add 1 cup of prunes. Divide into 3 layer cake pans. Bake at 350° for approximately 25 minutes or until the cake tests done.

In a saucepan combine the remaining eggs, brown sugar, margarine, cream, and prunes. Cook the mixture until thick. Spread between the layers and outside the cake. Let the cake stand overnight in an airtight container before cutting.

PINEAPPLE-DATE LOAF
10 servings

¼ cup butter, softened
½ cup sugar
1 egg
¼ teaspoon lemon extract
1 8½-ounce can crushed
  pineapple
¼ cup chopped pecans
2½ cups sifted all-purpose
  flour

2½ teaspoons baking powder
¼ teaspoon baking soda
1 teaspoon salt
½ cup finely chopped dates
¼ cup water
¼ cup chopped maraschino
  cherries

■ Cream together the butter and sugar. Add the egg and lemon extract. Drain the pineapple, reserving the liquid. Add the pineapple and the nuts to the creamed mixture. Sift together the dry ingredients. Add the dates to the dry ingredients and mix well to make sure the dates are coated. Stir the dry ingredients into the creamed mixture alternately with the reserved pineapple juice plus the water. Fold in the chopped maraschino cherries. Pour into a greased 9x5x3 loaf pan and bake at 375° for about 55 minutes or until the cake tests done.

YAM SPICE CAKE
8 to 10 servings

¾ cup butter, softened
2 cups packed brown sugar
4 eggs
2 tablespoons lemon juice
½ teaspoon vanilla extract
2½ cups all-purpose flour
1 teaspoon baking powder

1 teaspoon baking soda
1 teaspoon salt
1 teaspoon cinnamon
1 teaspoon nutmeg
1 cup mashed cooked yams
1 cup chopped nuts

■ Cream the butter and brown sugar until fluffy. Add the eggs, one at a time, mixing well after each addition. Beat in the lemon juice and vanilla. In a separate bowl sift together the flour, baking powder, soda, salt, and spices. Add to the creamed mixture alternately with the yams. Stir in the nuts and pour into a greased and floured 10-inch cake pan.

Bake at 300° for 1 hour and 20 minutes or until the cake tests done.

Buttermilk Frosting

1 cup sugar
1/2 teaspoon soda
1/4 cup butter

1/2 cup buttermilk
1 tablespoon light corn syrup
1 teaspoon vanilla extract

■ In a saucepan combine all of the ingredients and mix well. Bring to a boil, stirring constantly. Cook for 5 minutes. Pour over a warm cake.

Fudge Frosting

1/2 cup margarine
1/2 cup cocoa
2 cups sugar

1/2 cup milk
1 teaspoon vanilla extract

■ In a saucepan melt the margarine and add the other ingredients except the vanilla. Bring to a boil. Set the pan in cold water and beat until spreading consistency, then add the vanilla.

Honey-chocolate Frosting

1/2 cup butter
2 ounces unsweetened
  chocolate, cut up
1/2 cup sugar
1/8 teaspoon salt

1/3 cup honey
1/4 cup cream
2 egg yolks, slightly beaten

■ In a double boiler or heavy saucepan combine all of the ingredients except the egg yolks. When melted, blend the ingredients well. Stir about 3 tablespoons of the hot mixture into the egg yolks, and then add the egg yolks to the hot mixture. Cook, stirring constantly, for about 2 minutes, until slightly thickened. Place the pan in ice water and beat the frosting to spreading consistency.

APPLE PIE WITH CHEDDAR PASTRY
6 to 8 servings

1½ cups self-rising flour
1 tablespoon sugar
¼ teaspoon salt
⅜ cup shortening
1 cup shredded Cheddar
  cheese
¼ cup cold water

1 cup diced and pared apples
½ cup sugar
¼ teaspoon cinnamon
¼ teaspoon nutmeg
  Juice of 1 orange
2 teaspoons butter

■ Sift together the flour, sugar, and salt. Cut in the shortening, add the cheese, and mix well. Use just enough water to hold the dough together. Roll out onto a floured board and cut 2 inches larger than an inverted pie plate. Place in the pie plate. Spread the apples over the pastry and sprinkle with the sugar, cinnamon, and nutmeg. Squeeze the orange juice over the apples and dot with butter. Bake at 350° for 1 hour.

BUTTERMILK PIE

⅓ cup butter
1 cup sugar
3 egg yolks, beaten
3 tablepoons all-purpose
  flour
¼ teaspoon lemon juice

½ teaspoon grated lemon
  rind
1½ cups buttermilk
3 egg whites, stiffly beaten
1 unbaked 9-inch pie crust

■ Cream together the butter and sugar. Add the egg yolks and beat well. Add the flour, salt, lemon juice, and rind, and mix thoroughly. Add the buttermilk, and then fold in the beaten egg whites. Pour the filling into the crust and bake at 450° for 10 minutes. Reduce the heat to 350° and continue to bake for 40 minutes.

FUDGE PIE

2 ounces unsweetened
   chocolate
½ cup butter
2 eggs
1 cup sugar

2 tablespoons all-purpose
   flour
1 teaspoon vanilla extract
½ cup walnuts

■ In a double boiler or heavy saucepan melt the chocolate and butter. Add the eggs, sugar, flour, vanilla, and nuts. Bake in a greased pie pan at 325° for 30 minutes, starting in a cold oven.

GRANDMOTHER'S RAISIN CUSTARD PIE
6 to 8 servings

1 cup raisins
1 cup water
2 tablespoons butter
⅔ cup brown sugar
2 tablespoons all-purpose
   flour
2 eggs, separated

3 tablespoons lemon juice
1 baked 9-inch pie crust
¼ teaspoon cream of tartar
2 tablespoons sugar

■ Cook the raisins, water and butter to a boiling point. In a small bowl mix together the brown sugar and flour, and add to the raisin mixture. Gently add the 2 beaten egg yolks and stir over low heat until thickened. Add the lemon juice. Cool. Pour into baked pie crust. Beat the egg whites well. Add the cream of tartar and sugar and beat until dissolved. Cover the raisin mixture and bake at 350° for 12 minutes.

Lemon chess pie

5 egg yolks
1 tablespoon all-purpose flour
1 tablespoon cornmeal
2 cups sugar

1 cup milk
1/2 cup butter, melted
1 teaspoon lemon extract
1 unbaked 9-inch pie crust

■ Beat the egg yolks, adding the flour and cornmeal. Beat well, alternately adding the sugar, milk, and butter. Add the extract and bake at 350° for 1 hour.

Sweet potato pie
6 to 8 servings

3/4 cup sugar
1 teaspoon cinnamon
1/8 teaspoon cloves
1 teaspoon ginger
1/4 teaspoon salt
2 cups hot mashed sweet potatoes

2 tablespoons butter
3 eggs, beaten
1 1/4 cups milk
1 teaspoon grated lemon rind
1 unbaked 9-inch pie crust

■ Combine the sugar, cinnamon, cloves, ginger, and salt. Stir in the sweet potatoes and butter. Mix well and let cool. Beat in the eggs, and stir in the milk and lemon rind. Pour into the pie crust and bake at 400° for 40 to 50 minutes.

Pecan tassies
24 servings

1 3-ounce package cream cheese
1/2 cup butter, softened
1 cup all-purpose flour, sifted
2/3 cup pecan pieces, divided
1 egg

3/4 cup light brown sugar, firmly packed
1 tablespoon butter, softened
1 teaspoon vanilla extract
1/2 teaspoon salt

■ Combine the cream cheese and ½ cup butter. Add the flour and mix well. Chill for 1 hour. Shape the dough into 24 one-inch balls. Place in ungreased miniature 1¾-inch muffin tins. Press the bottom and sides to form tart shells. Divide ⅓ cup of the pecan pieces among pastry-lined cups. Prepare the filling by beating together the egg, sugar, butter, vanilla, and salt until smooth. Pour the egg mixture into the shells and top with the remaining pecans. Bake at 325° for 25 minutes. Cool and remove from the pans. These can be frozen after baking.

FRIED APPLE PIES
32 pies

1½ cups dried apples
3 cups water
¼ cup honey
2 tablespoons lemon juice
½ teaspoon grated lemon rind
½ teaspoon ground cinnamon
⅛ teaspoon salt
⅛ teaspoon ground nutmeg
3 cups unbleached flour, sifted
1 teaspoon salt
1 cup shortening
6 tablespoons cold water
1 quart oil

■ In a saucepan combine the apples and 3 cups of water. Bring to a boil, reduce the heat, cover and simmer for 35 minutes or until the apples are tender and the water is absorbed. Stir the apples until they are smooth and have no lumps. Add the honey, lemon juice, lemon rind, cinnamon, salt, and nutmeg. Mix well and set aside.

In a bowl combine the flour and salt. Cut in the shortening until crumbly, and sprinkle the remaining water over the surface until moistened. Shape into a ball and divide in half. Roll out on a floured surface. Cut with a 5-inch cutter. Place 1 tablespoon of apple filling on half of each circle, and fold over. Dampen the edges and seal with a fork. Keep the pies covered with a damp cloth until fried. Repeat until all of the dough is used.

In a 10-inch skillet heat 2 cups of oil to 375° and fry the pies until golden brown, turning as needed. Drain on paper towels. Add oil as needed.

GOOD LUCK PIE CRUST
2 9-inch double crust pie shells

4 cups all-purpose flour
1¾ cups shortening
1 tablespoon sugar
½ cup water

2 teaspoons salt
1 tablespoon vinegar
1 egg

■ With a fork mix together the flour, shortening, sugar, and water. In a separate bowl beat together the remaining ingredients. Combine the 2 mixtures and stir with a fork until moistened. By hand mold the dough into a ball and chill for 15 minutes. Roll into the desired shape.

BLACKBERRY COBBLER

⅔ cup shortening
2 cups sifted self-rising flour
4 tablespoons water
2 cups sugar

2 tablespoons cornstarch
4 cups blackberries
1 teaspoon lemon juice
½ cup butter

■ In a bowl cut half of the shortening into the flour until the mixture resembles coarse meal. Cut in the remaining shortening until the particles resemble large peas. Sprinkle with water and stir with a fork. Shape into a ball and wrap in waxed paper. Let the dough rest.

Reserve 2 tablespoons of sugar for the topping and combine the remaining sugar and cornstarch thoroughly. Add the fruit and lemon juice. Divide the dough in half and roll out in sections to fit a 2-quart dish, lining the bottom and sides. Pour the blackberries into the pastry lined dish. Dot with butter, reserving 2 tablespoons for the top. Bring the pastry over the fruit and dot with the remaining sugar and butter. Bake at 375° for 55 minutes.

OATMEAL-CHERRY COBBLER
6 servings

2 tablespoons cornstarch
3 tablespoons lemon juice
4 cups pitted cherries
¾ cup butter
1½ cups packed brown sugar

1½ cups all-purpose flour
½ teaspoon baking powder
½ teaspoon baking soda
1½ cups oatmeal
½ cup chopped walnuts

■ In a large bowl stir the cornstarch into the lemon juice and blend until smooth. Add the cherries, tossing to coat. Pour into a 9-inch square baking pan and set aside. In a medium skillet melt the butter. Cool slightly, and add the brown sugar. Add the remaining ingredients and mix well. Sprinkle over the cherries. Bake at 350° for 30 to 35 minutes, until golden brown.

RHUBARB COBBLER
6 servings

4 cups diced rhubarb
1 cup sugar
3 tablespoons butter
1½ cups all-purpose flour
¾ teaspoon salt

3 teaspoons baking powder
1 cup sugar
¼ cup shortening
1 egg, beaten
½ cup milk

■ Place the rhubarb in a greased 8x12-inch baking dish. Sprinkle with 1 cup of sugar and dot with butter. Heat at 350° while mixing the batter.

Sift together the remaining dry ingredients and cut in the shortening until the mixture resembles coarse crumbs. Mix the beaten egg with the milk and add to the flour mixture. Pour the batter over the hot rhubarb. Bake at 350° for 35 minutes, until browned. Serve warm.

HOT FUDGE PUDDING
6 servings

½ cup sifted all-purpose flour	¼ cup half and half
1 teaspoon baking powder	½ teaspoon vanilla
⅛ teaspoon salt	½ cup chopped walnuts
⅓ cup sugar	½ cup sifted brown sugar
3 tablespoons cocoa	⅞ cup boiling water
1 tablespoon butter, melted	Whipped cream

■ Combine the flour, baking powder, salt, sugar, and 1 tablespoon cocoa. Sift 3 times. Combine the butter, cream, and vanilla. Add the flour mixture and blend lightly. Stir in the nuts. Pour into a buttered 1-quart casserole. Combine the brown sugar and remaining cocoa. Sprinkle over the batter. Pour boiling water gently over all. Bake at 350° for 30 minutes. Serve with whipped cream.

MAMA'S RICE PUDDING
6 servings

1 cup uncooked rice	1 cup sugar
1½ cups water	1 cup milk
Dash salt	½ cup butter, melted
2 tablespoons butter	1 tablespoon vanilla extract
2 eggs	

■ Place the rice in a saucepan with the water, 2 tablespoons of butter, and a dash of salt. Bring to a boil, cover the saucepan, and allow the rice to simmer for 15 minutes or until the rice has absorbed all of the moisture.

In a mixing bowl, lightly beat the eggs. Add the sugar, milk, butter, and vanilla. Stir well and add to the rice mixture. Bake in an 8-inch baking dish at 350° for 15 minutes.

APPLE BROWN BETTY

6 servings

3 tablespoons butter
1½ cups bread crumbs
1 cup sugar
1½ teaspoons ground
   cinnamon

4½ cups sliced, pared, and
   cored apples
1 cup chopped walnuts

■ In a small saucepan melt the butter, and stir in the bread crumbs. Set aside. In a small bowl, combine the sugar with the cinnamon. Cover the bottom of a greased 1½-quart baking dish with part of the apple slices. Sprinkle with some of the sugar mixture, then walnuts, and the bread crumb mixture. Repeat the layers until all of the ingredients are used, ending with crumbs on top. Cover and bake at 350° for 30 minutes, then remove the cover and bake 15 more minutes to brown on top.

APPLE PAN DOWDY

6 green cooking apples,
   unpeeled
1 unbaked 9-inch 2-crust pie
   shell
½ cup sugar

½ teaspoon cinnamon
½ teaspoon cloves
⅛ teaspoon salt
4 tablespoons butter
½ cup molasses

■ Slice the apples and line the bottom of the pie crust. Sprinkle with the remaining ingredients. Top with lattice pastry. Bake at 350° for 45 minutes.

PEACH CRISP

½ cup butter
1 cup sugar
2 eggs
½ teaspoon nutmeg
½ teaspoon vanilla extract

1½ cups toasted bread cubes
2 cups corn flakes
4 cups peeled, sliced
   peaches
1 tablespoon lemon juice

■ Combine the butter and ½ cup of sugar and beat well. Beat in the eggs. Stir in the nutmeg, vanilla, bread cubes, and corn flakes. Spread half of this mixture in a buttered 1½-quart baking dish. Arrange the peaches over the mixture in the baking dish and sprinkle with the lemon juice and remaining sugar. Top with the remaining bread mixture. Bake at 375° for 20 minutes.

GINGER SNAP COOKIES
4 dozen

2 cups all-purpose flour
1 teaspoon baking soda
1 teaspoon cinnamon
1 teaspoon cloves
1 teaspoon ginger
¾ cup butter, softened
1 cup sugar
1 egg

¼ cup molasses
1½ tablespoons finely
   chopped crystalized
   ginger
1 cup raisins or dried
   currants
¾ cup chopped pecans
Sugar

■ Sift together the flour, baking soda, cinnamon, cloves, and ginger. Set aside. Cream together the butter and sugar until light and fluffy. Beat in the egg and molasses. Fold the dry ingredients into the butter mixture. Fold in the ginger, raisins, and pecans.
   Shape the dough 1 teaspoon at a time into balls. Coat in sugar, and press flat on a greased cookie sheet. Bake at 350° for 15 to 16 minutes, taking care not to let the cookies get too brown. Cool on racks. Store in an airtight container.

BROWN SUGAR DROPS
2 dozen

1/4 cup packed light brown
  sugar
1/4 cup butter
1/4 cup dark corn syrup

1/2 cup all-purpose flour
1 teaspoon ground ginger
1/8 teaspoon salt

■ In a large saucepan combine the brown sugar, butter, and corn syrup. Cook over low heat, stirring constantly, until the butter is melted. Remove from the heat. Stir in the flour, ginger, and salt until well blended. Drop by rounded teaspoons onto a greased and floured cookie sheet. Bake at 375° for 5 minutes or until the cookies are set.

COCONUT WASHBOARDS
20 cookies

3/4 cup unsalted butter, room
  temperature
1 cup packed dark brown
  sugar
1 egg
1 teaspoon vanilla extract
1/4 teaspoon almond extract

2 1/4 cups all-purpose flour
3/4 teaspoon baking powder
1/4 teaspoon cinnamon
1/4 teaspoon nutmeg
1/8 teaspoon salt
2 cups flaked coconut

■ In a large bowl cream together the butter and sugar. Beat in the egg until fluffy. Add the vanilla and almond extracts. Sift together the flour, baking powder, cinnamon, nutmeg, and salt and stir into the creamed mixture. Add the coconut, and blend well. Divide the dough in half and press each half into a rectangle on 2 baking sheets. Chill for 1 hour or until firm. Cut each rectangle into 10 rectangles and place 2 inches apart on a baking sheet. Score each with a fork to form ridges. Bake at 375° for 10 to 12 minutes, or until golden.

FRUITCAKE COOKIES
5 to 6 dozen

1 15-ounce box white
  raisins
1 pound candied pineapple,
  chopped
1 pound candied cherries,
  chopped
1½ pounds pecans
3 cups all-purpose flour
1 cup brown sugar

4 eggs, well beaten
½ cup margarine
1 teaspoon baking soda
½ teaspoon cinnamon
½ teaspoon nutmeg
½ cup white grape juice
1 teaspoon vanilla extract
3 tablespoons sour cream

■ Dredge the fruit and nuts well in 1 cup of the flour. In a large bowl beat the brown sugar, eggs, margarine, soda, spices, juice, vanilla, and sour cream together. Add the remaining flour, and combine with the fruit and nuts. Drop by teaspoons onto a greased baking sheet. Bake at 350° for 15 minutes or until done. Store in cloth soaked with grape juice in a covered tin container.

LEMON CORNMEAL COOKIES
3 dozen

1 cup butter, room
  temperature
1 cup sugar
2 egg yolks

1 teaspoon grated lemon
  peel
1½ cups all-purpose flour
1 cup yellow cornmeal

■ Beat the butter and sugar with a mixer until lighter in color and well blended. Add the egg yolks and mix well. Stir in the lemon peel, flour, and cornmeal to mix well. Wrap the dough and chill for 3 to 4 hours. Roll the dough on a lightly floured surface and cut into shapes. Place on an ungreased baking sheet and sprinkle with additional sugar. Bake in the center of the oven at 350° until the edges are browned.

MOLASSES COOKIES
1½ dozen

½ cup sugar
½ cup molasses
½ cup oil
½ cup hot water

2 teaspoons baking soda
2 teaspoons ginger
3¼ cups all-purpose flour

■ In a mixing bowl combine all of the ingredients and let stand for 10 minutes. Roll out the dough the size of a 10x15-inch cookie sheet, and place on the greased cookie sheet. Bake at 350° for 12 minutes or until done. Cut into squares.

OATMEAL COOKIES

1 cup sugar
½ cup butter
½ cup shortening
2 eggs
2 cups all-purpose flour
1 teaspoon baking powder
1 teaspoon salt

1 teaspoon cinnamon
1 teaspoon baking soda
½ cup warm water
2 cups quick-cooking oats
1 cup raisins
1 cup nuts, or more

■ Cream together the sugar, butter, and shortening. Add the eggs. Sift together the flour, baking powder, salt, and cinnamon, and add alternately with the soda dissolved in warm water to the creamed mixture. Mix thoroughly. Stir in the remaining ingredients and drop by teaspoons onto a greased baking sheet. Bake at 350° for 10 minutes or until done.

PEANUT BUTTER MACAROONS

2 egg whites
½ teaspoon vanilla extract
⅔ cup sugar
Dash salt

1 3½-ounce can
(1⅓ cups) flaked coconut
¼ cup peanut butter, melted
and cooled

■ Beat the egg whites, vanilla, sugar, and salt until soft peaks form. Fold in the coconut and melted peanut butter. Drop by rounded teaspoons onto a greased cookie sheet. Bake at 325° for 20 minutes.

PECAN THINS
8 dozen

1 cup butter
1 cup sugar
1 cup packed dark brown
sugar
1 egg
1 tablespoon vanilla extract

3 cups all-purpose flour
½ teaspoon baking powder
½ teaspoon baking soda
1½ cups finely chopped
pecans

■ In a large bowl cream the butter and gradually add the sugars, beating well. Add the egg and vanilla and beat until well blended. In a separate bowl combine the flour, baking powder, and soda. Gradually add to the creamed mixture, beating well after each addition. Stir in the pecans. Divide the dough in half and shape into rolls 1½-inch in diameter. Chill until firm. Thinly slice the dough and place the cookies on lightly greased cookie sheets. Bake at 350° for 12 minutes or until lightly browned.

APPLE CRUMB BARS
3 dozen

3 cups all-purpose flour
1 cup shortening
2 teaspoons baking powder
1 teaspoon salt
1 teaspoon vanilla extract
2 eggs

1 1/4 cups sugar
5 ounces apricot preserves
2 medium-sized cooking
  apples
1/4 teaspoon cinnamon or
  allspice

■ In a large bowl beat together the flour, shortening, baking powder, salt, vanilla, eggs, and 1 cup of sugar. Knead the dough until the mixture holds together. Reserve 1/4 cup of dough, and pat the remaining dough into a greased 13x9-inch pan. Spread the apricot preserves over the dough. Peel, core, and thinly slice the apples. Arrange the apple slices in rows over the preserves. Combine the cinnamon and 1/4 cup of sugar. Sprinkle over the apples. Crumble the reserved dough and sprinkle over the apples. Bake at 375° for 30 to 35 minutes, until golden.

BLACKBERRY BARS
1 dozen

1 cup all-purpose flour
3/4 cup packed brown sugar
1/4 cup butter or margarine
1/2 cup commercial sour
  cream
1 egg, beaten

3/4 teaspoon baking soda
1/4 teaspoon salt
1 teaspoon ground cinnamon
1/2 teaspoon vanilla extract
1 cup fresh blackberries
Sifted confectioners' sugar

■ Combine the flour and brown sugar. Cut in the butter until the mixture resembles coarse meal. Press 1 1/3 cups of the mixture into an ungreased 8-inch pan. Combine the remaining crumb mixture, sour cream, egg, baking soda, salt, cinnamon, and vanilla extract, and blend well. Stir in the blackberries, and spoon over the crust. Spread evenly. Bake at 350° for 35 minutes. Sprinkle with confectioners' sugar.

BROWN SUGAR BROWNIES
16 squares

½ cup butter
1 cup packed dark brown
  sugar
1 egg
½ teaspoon salt

1 cup all-purpose flour
1 teaspoon baking powder
½ teaspoon vanilla extract
½ cup chopped nuts

■ In a saucepan melt the butter and add the remaining ingredients. Spread in a buttered 8-inch pan. Bake at 350° for 25 minutes.

DOUBLE CHOCOLATE WALNUT BROWNIES
2 dozen squares

1 cup butter
4 ounces unsweetened
  chocolate
2 cups sugar
3 eggs
1 teaspoon vanilla extract

1 cup all-purpose flour,
  sifted
1½ cups coarsely chopped
  walnuts
1 6-ounce package
  semisweet chocolate
  pieces

■ In a heavy saucepan or double boiler melt the butter and chocolate. Remove from the heat and beat in the sugar. Add the eggs, vanilla, flour, and 1 cup of walnuts. Spread in a 13x9-inch pan. Combine the remaining walnuts with the chocolate pieces and sprinkle over the top of the cookie mixture, pressing lightly. Bake at 350° for 35 minutes.

CHOCOLATE OATMEAL CANDY
2 dozen squares

½ cup milk
2 cups sugar
½ cup margarine
4 tablespoons cocoa, sifted

2½ cups oatmeal
½ cup peanut butter
½ cup chopped nuts
2 teaspoons vanilla extract

■ In a saucepan boil the milk, sugar, margarine, and cocoa for 1½ minutes. Add the remaining ingredients, mix well, and pour into a greased pan. Cool at room temperature and cut into squares.

COFFEE CANDY

2 cups sugar
½ cup margarine
1 cup evaporated milk
1 12-ounce package
  semisweet chocolate pieces
1 7-ounce jar marshmallow
  creme

1 cup chopped nuts
1 tablespoon grated orange
  rind
1 tablespoon instant coffee
  granules
2 teaspoons orange flavoring

■ In a heavy saucepan combine the sugar, margarine, and milk. Bring to a boil, stirring constantly. Boil for 10 minutes, stirring constantly. Remove from the heat and stir in the chocolate pieces until melted. Add the marshmallow creme, nuts, orange rind, instant coffee, and orange flavoring. Beat until blended. Pour into a greased 13x9-inch pan. Cool at room temperature and cut into squares.

GRANDMOTHER'S FUDGE

2 cups sugar
¾ cup milk
2 1-ounce squares
  unsweetened chocolate

Dash salt
1 teaspoon corn syrup
2 tablespoons butter
1 teaspoon vanilla extract

■ Butter the sides of a heavy 2-quart saucepan, and combine the sugar, milk, chocolate, salt, and corn syrup in the greased saucepan. Cook over medium heat, stirring constantly, until the mixture comes to a boil. Cook to the soft-ball stage (234°), remove from the heat, and add the butter. Cool to 110° without stirring. Add the vanilla and beat the fudge until thick and no longer glossy, and spread in a greased shallow pan. Cut into squares when cool.

Molasses candy

2 cups sugar
2 cups sorghum molasses
2/3 cup water
1/4 teaspoon vinegar

1/4 cup butter
1/4 teaspoon salt
1/8 teaspoon baking soda

■ In a large saucepan combine the first 3 ingredients. Cook over medium heat to 265°. Remove from the heat and add the remaining ingredients. Pour onto a large platter or greased surface and let cool. When the candy is cool enough to handle, pull the candy until it becomes light in color. Drop onto a greased surface.

Nannie's holiday candy

3 cups sugar
1 cup corn syrup
1 1/2 cups cream
1/2 pound Brazil nuts
1/2 pound walnuts

1/2 pound pecans
1/2 pound candied cherries
1/2 pound candied pineapple

■ In a large saucepan cook the sugar, corn syrup, and cream to the soft-ball stage (234°). Beat immediately until thick and gooey. Add the nuts and candied fruit. Pack into a greased baking dish and chill for 24 hours. Slice to serve.

Peanut brittle

3 cups sugar
1 cup white corn syrup
1 cup water
1 pound shelled raw peanuts

1/4 teaspoon salt
1 teaspoon vanilla extract
2 tablespoons butter
1 tablespoon baking soda

■ Cook the sugar, syrup, and water to the hard ball stage (250°). Add the peanuts and continue cooking until slightly caramelized (300°). Remove from the heat, and add the salt, vanilla, butter, and soda. Stir until frothy and pour onto a warm, buttered cookie sheet. When cool, break into pieces.

PRALINES
20 servings

1 cup packed light brown
  sugar
½ cup sugar
½ cup milk

¼ cup light corn syrup
1 teaspoon vanilla extract
¼ cup margarine
1 cup pecan pieces

■ In a saucepan combine the brown sugar, sugar, milk, and corn syrup. Stir until the sugar dissolves, cooking slowly. Boil to the soft ball stage (238°). Remove from the heat and add the vanilla and margarine. Beat until the mixture thickens. Add the pecans and continue to beat. Drop by teaspoons onto waxed paper.

SPICED PECANS

1 egg white
2½ tablespoons water
¾ cup sugar
1 teaspoon cinnamon
¼ teaspoon nutmeg

¼ teaspoon allspice
¼ teaspoon ground cloves
¾ teaspoon salt
3 cups shelled pecans

■ Beat the egg white and water until frothy. Add the remaining ingredients except the pecans and blend well. Stir in the pecans gently to avoid breaking and coat well. Remove the pecans from the egg mixture and place on a foil-covered cookie sheet. Spread in a thin layer, keeping the pecans from touching as much as possible. Bake at 275° for 45 minutes, stirring gently after 20 minutes. Stir again 15 minutes later. Spread on waxed paper to cool, keeping the pecans from touching. Store in an airtight container.

Index